The Community Networking Handbook

WITHDRAWN

STEPHEN T. BAJJALY

AMERICAN LIBRARY ASSOCIATION
Chicago and London
1999

While extensive effort has gone into ensuring the reliability of information appearing in this book, the publisher makes no warranty, express or implied, on the accuracy or reliability of the information, and does not assume and hereby disclaims any liability to any person for any loss or damage caused by errors or omissions in this publication.

Project editor: Louise D. Howe

Cover and text design by Todd Sanders.

Composition by The Publishing Services Group in Minion using QuarkXpress 3.3 on a Macintosh platform.

Printed on 50-pound white offset, a pH-neutral stock, and bound in 10-point coated cover stock by McNaughton & Gunn.

The paper used in this publication meets the minimum requirements of American National Standard for Information Sciences—Permanence of Paper for Printed Library Materials, ANSI Z39.48-1992. ∞

Library of Congress Cataloging-in-Publication Data

Bajjaly, Stephen T.
   The community networking handbook / by Stephen T. Bajjaly.
      p.   cm.
   Includes bibliographical references and index.
   ISBN 0-8389-0745-8
   1. Libraries and community—United States—Data processing.
   2. Electronic villages (Computer networks)—United States.
   3. Community information services—United States—Data processing.
   4. Libraries and electronic publishing—United States.   5. Libraries
   and community—Canada—Data processing.   6. Electronic villages
   (Computer networks)—Canada.   7. Community information
   services—Canada—Data processing.   8. Libraries and electronic
   publishing—Canada.   I. Title.
   Z716.4.B24   1999
   021.2'0285—dc21   98-45246

Printed in the United States of America.

03 02 01 00 99   5 4 3 2 1

To My Parents

DR. FLOYD LOUIS BAJJALY
NORA WILSON TROUP BAJJALY

Two outstanding role models whose love,
integrity, generosity, hard work,
and enthusiasm for knowledge have
encouraged me always

Contents

Preface

For the past decade, cities and towns the world over have established community computer systems—called community networks—to help people and organizations negotiate the transition from the paper-based world we know so well to the online, electronic, networked world of the future. Today every community can easily connect to the Internet so that distant people and locals alike can tap into a database of local information, communicate with one another, and experience almost firsthand the benefits a particular community has to offer. With this worldwide connectivity, even the smallest, most rural community can become an important part of the burgeoning "global village." Every community can compete on a global scale. To do so, every community can—and must—tell its version of the same story: Why is this community a great place to live and work?

I wrote this book because I see considerable untapped potential for community networking initiatives—whether already up-and-running or yet to be started—to benefit from the full participation of the local library. While this book is designed to be useful to anyone wanting to put his or her community fully online, my message is aimed squarely at librarians: community networking needs you! As I write this, there are about 215 established community networks in the United States and Canada. Less than one third identify a library as a major partner. And yet I wonder: What institution does the community rely on most of all for information? What institution knows more about how to organize material so that it is easy to find? What institution offers more free public space where people can congregate? What institution has more technology and shares it with the public?

My fear is that sometime in the future local officials will get the brilliant idea to establish another government agency: "The Office of Electronic Information." This office will be charged with collecting, organizing, and electronically disseminating information about every aspect of life in the community, providing public access to this information, and making sure every citizen can find what he or she needs.

Tax dollars will be diverted to fund this new agency. New staff will be recruited. All the while, the local librarians will be scratching their heads wondering why no one realized they could (and often already do) provide these important services.

I hope this book will inspire librarians to meet the challenge of community networking. After all, nobody will say this is easy. It will, however, allow you to apply your valuable skills in whole new ways and to help ensure the long-run future of your library. Community networking needs your understanding of information organization, retrieval, and access; your strongly held views on censorship, first amendment rights, and universal access; and your willingness and capability to help all members of the community improve their information literacy skills and meet their information needs.

This book is designed to help you take a proactive stance toward delivering community networking services in your community. This book will help you to conceptualize community networking initiatives that make sense for your community by giving you an overview of the issues and activities you might consider. Throughout the book I alert you to helpful organizations and valuable resources—both in print and online—to consult. Since every community is unique, "one size fits all" solutions don't really work. My goal is to point you in the right direction and, above all else, save you time. With this book you will be able to put your effort where it will count the most: developing and delivering important twenty-first century information services for your community.

My personal interest in community networking dates to 1993 when I joined the faculty of the College of Library and Information Science at the University of South Carolina. We wanted to support a university-wide community outreach initiative. But how? We quickly hit on the notion of starting a community network. We had seen a promotional video about the Heartland FreeNet in which local residents were given electronic access to one another and to lots of local information. We were excited about how community networking services could strengthen the public library and about how a working community network could provide our students with wonderful new learning opportunities.

Over the next few months, more and more participants—both inside and outside the university—joined our brainstorming sessions about how to start one of these networks in our community. Our efforts were greatly boosted in 1994 when we were one of ten cities nationwide to be awarded a $109,000 grant from the Corporation for

Public Broadcasting (CPB). The Community-Wide Education and Information System (CWEIS) Project was the first grant program ever to fund community networking projects specifically. For details on the completed CWEIS projects, consult the CPB Web site:

www.cpb.org/edtech/cweis/projects.html

The College of Library and Information Science, along with our project partners (the University's Computer Services Division, South Carolina Educational Television, and the Richland County Public Library), set to work to implement our community network. MidNet, the community network for Columbia and the Midlands of South Carolina, was born on Valentine's Day 1995! In addition to my ongoing duties as a faculty member, I became MidNet's Project Director. I am proud to say that not only did we forge a unique partnership among three large educational institutions, but we offered public access across all ten branches of the public library from Day One.

For the next eighteen months, with the help of one full-time staff person, a few graduate assistants, and lots of student interns and volunteers, MidNet put over seventy-five local organizations online, trained over five hundred people in how to use online information services, and provided free online accounts to over ten thousand people. While we have been unable to sustain much of this effort beyond the grant period, MidNet remains a valuable learning laboratory for our students and an important resource for an ever-increasing number of local community agencies. Please "drop by" and take a look:

www.midnet.sc.edu

I welcome your ideas, comments, thoughts, and suggestions. Like everything related to the Internet, community networking continues to evolve at a dizzying pace. To make your job a bit easier, hyperlinks to the online resources mentioned throughout this book, as well as to additional pertinent resources, are available through my Web site:

www.libsci.sc.edu/stephen/bajjaly.htm

Acknowledgments

I began the research for this book by interviewing many librarians and other individuals about their community networking activities and experiences. I want to thank each of them for their time and suggestions:

Audrey Bangert
St. Charles City-County Library District, St. Peters, Missouri

Elinor Barrett
Daniel Boone Regional Library, Columbia Online Information Network (COIN), Missouri

Sue Beckwith
Austin Free-Net, Austin, Texas

Tammy Benshoof
University of Tennessee-Knoxville and KORRNET, Knoxville, Tennessee

Wally Bowen
Mountain Area Information Network, Asheville, North Carolina

Frank Bridge
Austin Public Library, Austin, Texas

Jim Brown
St. Charles City-County Library District, Westplex Information Network (WIN), St. Peters, Missouri

Margaret Bruni
Detroit Public Library, Detroit, Michigan

Annie Busch
Springfield-Greene County Library and ORION, Springfield, Missouri

Tony Carmack
Medina County Free-Net, Medina, Ohio

Yvonne Chen
Seattle Public Library, Seattle, Washington

Janet Drumheller
Knox County Public Library, Knoxville, Tennessee

Jeanne Duffey
Ozarks Regional Information Online Network (ORION), Springfield, Missouri

Andrea Ellinor
Software Solutions Now!, Tallahassee, Florida

Kimberley Vendrick Evans
Montgomery-Floyd Regional Library, Christiansburg, Virginia

Dave Farley
Mayor's Office, City of Pittsburgh, Pennsylvania

Becky Gadell
Austin City Connection, Austin, Texas

Marlene Harris
Evanston Public Library, Evanston, Illinois

Tracy Harris
Community Access Program, Industry Canada, Ottawa, Ontario, Canada

Steve Helm
Montgomery-Floyd Regional Library, Christiansburg, Virginia

Susan Holmes
Three Rivers Free-Net and Carnegie Library of Pittsburgh, Pittsburgh, Pennsylvania

Bonnie Howard
Medina County Free-Net, Medina, Ohio

Rick Hulsey
Willard Public Library, Great Lakes Free-Net, Battle Creek, Michigan

Dan Iddings
Carnegie Library of Pittsburgh, Pittsburgh, Pennsylvania

Ann King
Westplex Information Network (WIN), St. Peters, Missouri

Virginia Kneisner
Austin Public Library, Austin, Texas

Jane Kolbe
South Dakota State Library, Pierre, South Dakota

Herb Kyles
Community Resource Network, Kansas City, Kansas

Hilbert Levitz
Tallahassee Free-Net, Tallahassee, Florida

Gary Linden
Medina County Free-Net, Medina, Ohio

Helen Moeller
Leon County Public Library, Tallahassee, Florida

Maggie Preiss
St. Charles City-County Library District, Westplex Information Network (WIN), St. Peters, Missouri

Jane Rosenfeld
Buffalo and Erie County Public Library and Buffalo Free-Net, Buffalo, New York

Michael Rouse
Leon County Public Library, Tallahassee Free-Net, Tallahassee, Florida

Dana Ruby
South Dakota State Library, Pierre, South Dakota

Peggy Rueda
Boulder Community Network, Boulder, Colorado

Carl Sandstedt
St. Charles City-County Library District, St. Peters, Missouri

Bob Smith
Medina County Library, Medina, Ohio

Anna Sylvan
St. Charles City-County Library District, St. Peters, Missouri

Cynthia Terwilliger
University of Michigan, Ann Arbor, Michigan

Kevin Tharp
Ozarks Regional Information Online Network (ORION), Springfield, Missouri

Mary Virnoche
Boulder Community Network, Boulder, Colorado

Tony Wening
Missouri Research and Education Network (MoreNet), Springfield, Missouri

Sam Werberg
Austin Free-Net, Austin, Texas

John Wolforth
Community Computer Consultant, Minneapolis, Minnesota

Neil Yerkey
SUNY–Buffalo and Buffalo Free-Net, Buffalo, New York

I owe special thanks to the following individuals for contributing written materials that I have quoted or adapted: Sue Beckwith, Steve Cisler, Joan Durrance, Kim Gregson, Terry Grunwald, Cindi Hickey, Susan Holmes, Jamie McClelland, Peter Morgan, Mario Morino, David Murdoch, Frank Odasz, Doug Schuler, Gwen Simpson, Deborah Snow, Craig Stillings, Mary Virnoche, and Joan Waldron.

I learned a tremendous amount from participants at the Community Technology Centers Network (CTCNet), American Library Association, and Telecommunities Canada conferences held during the summer of 1997.

There are several individuals whose support and encouragement enabled me to complete this book: my best friend, Jerry Evans, for encouraging me to undertake this project; many other friends and family members (my dad especially!) for inquiring regularly about my progress; Dr. Thomas Galvin, my mentor and faculty advisor at SUNY–Albany; my Dean, Fred Roper, and my colleagues and students at the University of South Carolina College of Library and Information Science; and Benjamin Breazeale, Carolyn McClendon, and everyone else associated with MidNet. Finally, I owe special thanks to my editors, Patrick Hogan, Louise Howe, and Libby Rubenstein, and to others at ALA Editions for their insight and helpful comments on this manuscript.

The Importance of Community Networking

In the broadest sense, community networking means effectively applying information and information technologies to improve the lives of local residents—the neighbors, friends, associates, colleagues, employees, bosses, students, teachers, patrons, customers, constituents, parishioners with whom you physically interact everyday. Although these networks are as unique as the communities they serve, all share two common objectives. As the world has begun to connect electronically in a big way, community networks have extended this online access to community-specific information. Secondly, community networks encourage anyone and everyone to participate.

Every community—urban or rural, big or small—has a story to tell. As we move increasingly into an electronically driven world, this story needs to be told online. Parts of the story are useful mainly to the people who physically reside in the community: When is the trash picked up? How do I obtain a business license? What decisions were reached at last night's county council meeting? Who is the high school football team playing this week? Other parts of the story may appeal to people the world over: What is the local history? What are the sightseeing points of interest? How about the best places to eat, drink, shop, and sleep? What makes this community unique?

The continuing evolution of computers and telecommunications makes it ever easier and more affordable to deliver round-the-clock, fully interactive, electronic information services that positively affect us all. Over time, community networking has evolved, too, into more a process than a product. These systems no longer represent the only way for average citizens to connect online. Yet community networks remain an important strategy for the community's institutions to collaborate on the delivery of local online information services.

The integration of computers further and further into our everyday lives continues unabated as it has since the advent of the microprocessor over twenty-five years ago. The microprocessor—a transistor-packed silicon chip about the size of a quarter—is changing our lives more profoundly than anyone anticipated or could have imagined just a few years ago. For the microprocessor is central to a new era, the "Information Age."

The Information Age means a burgeoning global economy with information as the critical commodity. The technologies that enable us to create, manipulate, and use information are critically important. The ability to use a computer is increasingly assumed—and required. In the Information Age, rapidly changing technologies have become a fact of life—a fact we have to embrace whether we like it or not. Time and geographic location are no longer limitations.

In this era of global markets and global competition, more and more work is information related: the United States has shifted away from manufacturing toward service and knowledge work. Today two-thirds of American workers are in information-related jobs such as sales and marketing, professional services, education, financial services, government, or customer service. The rest rely heavily on information.

The Information Age has brought more competition and downsizing to the workplace than ever before. The result: the work world is vastly different from what it was just a few years ago. The size of the effective organization has shrunk severely. Today's effective organizations are flatter and resemble a web—just like the computer networks upon which they depend. Today, all employees must constantly demonstrate how they add value to the organization. Gone are the days when your title determined your power. Now it is what you know that counts. And knowing how to access, process, and apply information are increasingly critical skills.

More recently, organizations of all sizes and computer-literate people of all ages and from all walks of life are learning about and trying the next logical step: going online. The increasing use of the Internet and online information services means that people are relying on computers now as much for communication as for computation. More and more people every day are using this most modern technology to engage in the most ancient human pursuit: connecting with one another.

While the costs associated with computing continue to drop and the number of people who can effectively use a computer continues to increase, we are a long way from realizing the full benefits of the Information Age. Too many of our citizens have never touched a computer, much less learned how to use one effectively. To many, going online and experiencing its benefits remain vague concepts with little significance or practical application to daily life. As profound and as wonderful as all this can be, too many of our fellow citizens are being left "out of the loop"—and the long-run consequences could be grave.

The NII and Telecommunications Policy

The phenomenal growth of the Internet—the confluence of computers and communications—is but the latest evidence that we are undergoing a telecommunications revolution that began with the government breakup of the Bell System in the mid-1980s. Historically, governments the world over have viewed telecommunications as part of the social infrastructure (like roads). Until recently the telecommunications industry in every country was a regulated monopoly. With the advent of a global economy driven by access to information, this position has undergone some serious rethinking. Significant changes in laws, regulations, and policies are intended to foster competition by decreasing the amount of government oversight. It is believed that true competition in the telecommunications industry will greatly benefit consumers and nations as a whole by providing increased services at more competitive rates.

In the United States, an agenda for developing a "National Information Infrastructure" was proposed by President Clinton early in his administration (September 1993).[1] The NII was envisioned as a seamless web of communications networks, computers, databases, and consumer electronics that would put vast amounts of information at users' fingertips. The President's Agenda emphasized that all Americans have a stake in the construction of an advanced NII. With a national information infrastructure in place:

People would be free to live almost anywhere they want—without forgoing opportunities for useful and fulfilling employment by "telecommuting" to work over the "electronic highway"

The best schools, teachers, and courses would be available to all students—without regard to geography, distance, resources, or disability

Social services would be available online, when and where people need them

The federal government was designated to play a leadership role, but the private sector will build and run the NII. While there has been plenty of hype about telecommunications and technology, the passage in 1996 of the Telecommunications Reform Act was expected to foster competition and to bring about the most sweeping changes in our communications and information industries since the Communications Act of 1934. The World Trade Organization Agreement, reached in 1997, is designed to do the same on an international level. According to Susan Ness, a federal communications commissioner, one thing can be said for sure: The Internet will dramatically alter the communications and information industries. Established companies and entrepreneurs alike see enormous opportunities in trying to satisfy the need for ever-increasing bandwidth at prices we can afford.[2]

A major objective of the President's plan was to extend the concept of universal service to the information needs of the American people in the twenty-first century. The NII agenda describes universal service as a process of eliminating barriers so that everyone would have the opportunity to use our telecommunications system for meaningful and effective participation in all aspects of the information society of the twenty-first century. That is, the NII should provide all interested Americans with easy, affordable access to advanced communication and information services without regard to income, disability, or location.

While the 1996 Telecommunications Reform Act considerably narrows the concept of universal service, the Snowe-Rockefeller Amendment ensures that discounted rates for telecommunications services will be available to schools and libraries when used for educational purposes. To pay for the discounts, starting in 1998 a new universal service fund is being established and funded at $2.25 billion per year. Telecommunications carriers will pay into this fund based on their annual sales. Schools and libraries that want to tap into the fund will submit a technology plan describing the information services they would provide with the discounted telecommunications services and products.

Commonly referred to as the "E-rate," the discounts will apply to telecommunications services, internal connections, and Internet access. That is, discount rates will apply to the purchase of hubs, routers, file servers, and wireless LANs but, unfortunately, will not help to provide computers, training, or software. The amount of the discount (off of the prevailing price) to which a school or library is entitled will be based upon the local poverty rate, as measured by the number of children eligible for subsidized school lunches. While it remains to be seen if this is an adequate means to ensure universal service, it should ensure that schools and libraries remain pivotal to delivering these services to their communities in the years ahead.[3]

Community Networking Goals

The same phenomena affecting organizations and individuals apply to our communities. After all, what else are communities made of? Smart, forward-thinking communities have realized a basic fact of the Information Age: providing citizens with electronic access to information and ensuring that they have the necessary skills to make use of this information improves both the quality of life for residents and the economic development potential of the community.

With the Internet as the underlying information transport mechanism, a community that goes online can provide the same access to information seekers across town or across the globe. The "connected" community enables far-off people to experience almost firsthand the benefits it has to offer. With this worldwide connectivity, even the smallest, most rural community can become an important part of the burgeoning "global village." Communities that make electronic information access a public priority will have competitive advantages over those that do not. In this age of information, the ability to find, access, and use information resources makes businesses more competitive, individuals more marketable, and the community more desirable.

To make electronic information access a public priority requires the community to focus on three important aspects:

Equity—the same information must be available to everyone

Decentralization—the information must be accessible in a variety of locations

Collaboration—information delivery must be coordinated to ensure that information seekers can get one simple, straight, accurate answer to their questions, concerns, or problems

Community networking is a process designed to achieve the necessary electronic information access objectives in order to improve the quality of life and the economic development of the community. These objectives include:

Developing important and useful electronic information resources and services focused on the local community, such as cultural events, business, community organizations, education, government, health, libraries, media and news, sports and recreation, transportation, and the weather

Providing affordable access to these electronic resources and services throughout the community

Offering the necessary level of training, support and technical assistance so that every individual and organization in the community can participate

A community network applies modern computer and communications technologies to provide low-cost online information services and access to information for and about the community that is not available online from any other source.[4] While a community network is based upon technology, its success rests with its people—organizers, public officials, information providers, sponsors, users, volunteers—who support the network in a variety of ways. A community network makes a statement about the community it serves, and in a sense defines a community both to its own citizens and to the rest of the electronic world. Through the network, the community can gain access to global resources, and the rest of the world can electronically explore the community.

Most importantly, a community network can reignite a spirit of cooperation and belonging that we thought was lost forever. The network provides a way to unite the efforts of school districts, libraries, local government, and other agencies to support public access to information and reinforce a stronger sense of community. Further, the network can build upon the efforts of local information providers already online and help new information providers to get online.

In a recent study, the RAND Corporation, a public policy think tank, found that the gap between those using computer technology and those who are not is growing each year. And this is the case despite lower costs of equipment and greater general awareness. The RAND Corporation study highlights community networking as a positive strategy to counteract the growing computer literacy gap because a community network exists to meet the needs of the general public, to increase public access to information, and to serve traditionally underserved members of the community.[5]

We must ensure a level playing field between the "haves" and the "have nots": those who have access to technology and those who do not. These underserved members of the community include those who are poor, uneducated, members of minority groups, elderly, or those with disabilities. But providing access to technology to these groups is not sufficient. We must further ensure that no discrepancy exists between those who are computer literate and those who are not: the so-called cans and cannots. This is especially important as more and more information goes online and may not be available in any other format. As Sue Beckwith, former executive director of the Austin Free-Net, says, "Disparity has always existed. But with these new technologies, it is increasing at an increasing rate. We keep asking: What are we doing in Austin, Texas, to mitigate these problems?"[6]

The History of Community Networking

Community networking dates to 1984 and the work of Tom Grundner at Case Western Reserve University in Cleveland, Ohio. Grundner, using a small computer and a single modem line, established an online bulletin board dubbed "St. Silicon's Hospital and Information Dispensary." His goal was to test the effectiveness of online access as a way to deliver health information to the general public. Local citizens were able to dial into St. Silicon's, leave medically related questions, and receive an answer from a board-certified physician within a day.

This experiment proved so successful that Grundner secured enough funding to start a full-scale "community computer system" to provide free e-mail to the people around Cleveland and electronic information in areas as diverse as law, medicine, education, the arts, science, and government. In July 1986, this system, known as the Cleveland Free-Net, went online. Over the next three years, the Cleveland Free-Net registered over seven thousand users and handled between five and six hundred calls per day. A second system, the Youngstown Free-Net, began operation in July 1987. Over the next couple of years, three more systems became operational: TriState Online in Cincinnati, Ohio; the Heartland Free-Net in Peoria, Illinois; and the first rural system, the Medina County Free-Net in Medina, Ohio.

In 1989, the concept of a community computer system was expanded and formalized and the National Public Telecomputing Network (NPTN) was born. The goal of NPTN was to help new systems come online and to support them afterward with services and information resources. Today, well over two hundred communities in the United States and Canada host their own community networks. Although Grundner is no longer a visible part of the community networking movement and NPTN is no longer a functioning organization, I believe his early words provide a lasting legacy that remains true today even though much in the world of computing has changed:

> First, it is clear that these community computers represent the leading edge of what can only be described as a new telecommunications medium. Telecomputing is not radio, not television, not print, but has characteristics of all three plus additional characteristics all its own. This fact alone will inevitably lead to developments and uses that we cannot now even begin to imagine.
>
> Second, it is clear that a critical mass of people now exists who are prepared to utilize this new medium. As more and more modem-equipped microcomputers penetrate the home and especially the work environment, the utility of public-access computerized information services goes up.
>
> And third, there is a certain sense of inevitability to the development of community computing. Simply stated, we find ourselves unable to imagine a twenty-first century in which we do not have community computer systems, just as this century had the free public library. Moreover, we believe that the community computer, as a resource, will have at least as much impact on the next century as the public library has had on ours.
>
> Most people do not realize that in the latter part of the last century there was no such thing as the free public library, at least not as we know it today. Eventually the literacy rate became high enough (and the cost of books became cheap enough) that the public library became feasible. People in cities and towns all across the country banded together to make

free public access to the printed word a reality. The result was a legacy from which virtually every person has benefited.

In this century, we believe we have reached the point where computer "literacy" has gotten high enough (and the cost of equipment low enough) that a similar demand has formed for free, public access, computerized information systems. Indeed, we believe we have reached a point where the question is no longer whether it will happen; the question is "who" and "when." Who will do it and when will it happen?[7]

There are many reasons why a community should establish a community network:

To satisfy the basic information needs of the community

To build a platform for local agencies to make their information easily available in an electronic format

To deliver local public information in an easily accessible format

To improve community collaboration through joint efforts and resource sharing

To provide a powerful tool for community economic development and tourism

To promote and encourage individual lifelong education

To give citizens access points to information available beyond the community

To expand the knowledge base of the citizens of the community

To ensure universal access to electronic information

To create opportunities for children and adults to expand their awareness, develop friendships, and trade ideas with others in their community, their state, their country, and the global society

To facilitate communications between citizens and their elected representatives and government agencies

To prepare the citizens of the community for full participation in the rapidly emerging information-based economy

Even to people who deal with computers every day, the continually accelerating pace of technological change is daunting. Community networking represents an important strategy in our nation's quest to provide universal access to information. This quest began with the advent of the public library over a century ago. It remains a cornerstone of our democracy as we build the information infrastructure that will support us in the twenty-first century. The next chapter describes the full range of community networking services and discusses why community networking is so important to libraries.

For More Information

A number of books have been published in the past few years that address the future of the Information Age and the role of the Internet. For reviews of these and other related titles, I recommend you consult the online bookstore, Amazon.com (www.amazon.com), or a similar source.

Computerization and Controversy: Value Conflicts and Social Choices, 2nd Edition, edited by Rob Kling. San Diego, Calif.: Academic Press, 1996. ISBN: 0124150403.

Cyberspace: The Human Dimension, by David B. Whittle. New York: W. H. Freeman, 1997. ISBN: 0716783118.

The Death of Distance: How the Communications Revolution Will Change Our Lives, by Frances Cairncross. Cambridge, Mass.: Harvard Business School Press, 1997. ISBN: 0875848060.

Growing Up Digital: The Rise of the Net Generation, by Don Tapscott. New York: McGraw-Hill, 1997. ISBN: 0070633614.

Interface Culture: How New Technology Transforms the Way We Create and Communicate, by Steven Johnson. San Francisco: HarperSanFrancisco, 1997. ISBN: 0062514822.

Internet Culture, edited by David Porter. New York: Routledge, 1997. ISBN: 0415916844.

Release 2.0: A Design for Living in the Digital Age, by Esther Dyson. New York: Broadway Books, 1997. ISBN: 0767900111.

Resisting the Virtual Life: The Culture and Politics of Information, edited by James Brook and Ian A. Boal. San Francisco: City Lights Books, 1995. ISBN: 0872862992.

War of the Worlds: Cyberspace and the High-Tech Assault on Reality, by Mark Slouka. New York: Basic Books, 1996. ISBN: 0465004873.

What Will Be: How the New World of Information Will Change Our Lives, by Michael L. Dertouzos and Bill Gates. San Francisco: HarperSanFrancisco, 1997. ISBN: 0062514792.

NOTES

1. *The National Information Infrastructure Agenda for Action,* White House Press Releases Database. (www.whitehouse.gov/WH/html/ library.html)
2. "From Hype to Reality in the Emerging Digital Age," speech by Susan Ness, Wall Street Journal Technology Summit, October 15, 1997. (www.fcc.gov/Speeches/ Ness/spsn721.html)
3. See the E-Rate Hotline (www.eratehotline.org/) or the FCC Universal Service Home Page (www.fcc.gov/ccb/universal_service/welcome.html) for more information.
4. Some material in this section is adapted from the Missouri Express Web Site (outreach.missouri.edu/moexpress/). Used with permission. Missouri Express is sponsored by the Office of Administration, State of Missouri, and is a joint project of the Missouri Research and Education Network (MOREnet), University Outreach and Extension, Missouri Department of Economic Development, and the Missouri Association of Councils of Government.
5. *Universal Access to E-Mail: Feasibility and Societal Implications,* by Robert H. Anderson, Tora K. Bikson, Sally Ann Law, and Bridger M. Mitchell. 1995. (www. rand.org/publications/MR/MR650/)
6. Sue Beckwith, communication to the author.
7. Tom Grundner, communication to the author.

2

Why Libraries Should Participate

Community networking offers those of us in the information professions a way to draw on what we know in order to give back something new and critically important to our communities. One of our profession's most important responsibilities as we embark on a new century is to help our communities deal effectively with the Information Age. We must seize the opportunity to catalyze professionals and nonprofessionals alike to ensure that everyone in our communities has an equal opportunity to participate in—and benefit from—the products and services, opportunities and advantages, which a fully networked, electronic world may bring.

Although community networking is a relatively new concept that takes energy and effort, a great synergy can develop between the library and the community network. A community network offers the library (as well as other community-based institutions) an important strategy to demonstrate its continuing relevance in today's society. Community networking enables the library to reach out to new constituents and deliver new services. Community networking enables a broad base of community institutions to work cooperatively; to share knowledge, skills, and capabilities; and to communicate their positive interest and attitude about the future well-being of the community. Community networking enables these institutions to move their communities squarely into the Information Age and, thereby, to improve not only the community's overall economic development potential but the quality of life for all its residents—current and future.

As we become more a part of a global economy, the continuing relevance of every community institution to our future society is currently in question. Each must demonstrate how it adds value in the competitive world of today. For instance:

Local government is under pressure from taxpayers to reduce the costs of government while, at the same time, providing an increased level of service and being more customer service oriented.

Managed care and hospital consolidation are changing the way we look at health care and medical costs. Health care marketing is a booming industry.

School problems are constantly in the news. Almost everyone thinks our public education system is a mess. Despite evidence to the contrary, the public school is under constant attack for not doing enough to educate our children. Standardized test scores are not acceptable. Crimes committed by children and teen pregnancy are on the rise. Violence in schools is a phenomenon unheard of just a few years ago.

Why should the library be immune from these changes? Community networking provides a real "win-win" opportunity for the public library and for every other community institution. While helping the community address an issue of critical importance, community networking provides its sponsoring institutions with a plan, a method, a strategy to ensure their continued relevance in the Information Age.

Community networking provides opportunities for other types of libraries to become involved, too. For instance, state and provincial libraries can serve an important advocacy role with government political and administrative leaders; can offer centralized equipment, training, and technical support to the local communities within their jurisdictions; and can develop templates of products and services for their local public libraries to implement. Academic libraries, in concert with their affiliated colleges and universities, can assist with the development and implementation of newly available "cutting-edge" technologies and with measuring and evaluating the impact of community networking services. Special libraries can financially support the expansion of community networking services into disadvantaged parts of the community.

Even though it remains extremely difficult to predict the future, one fact seems certain: information will be an increasingly critical commodity and institutions that deliver it have an opportunity to be a part of this future. So, in essence, community networking gives the institutions in the community a way to deal with change.

> Change involves the crystallization of new action possibilities (new policies, new behaviors, new patterns, new methodologies, new products, or new market ideas) based on reconceptualized patterns in the organization. The architecture of change involves the design and construction of new patterns, or the reconceptualization of old ones, to make new, and hopefully more productive, actions possible.[1]

Community networking means taking advantage of the new computer and telecommunications technologies to deliver new information services and enable the community's information providers to cooperate in new and different ways to enhance the capacity of the community. So, if you want to conceptualize community networking in your community, think of it as a way for your institution to invest in the future of the community. Think of it as a strategy to increase community capacity.

The library is the natural leader of the community networking effort. After all, what other community institution knows more about delivering information services? What other community institution has a better grasp on the current state of affairs in the community? Of course, other community institutions probably know more about their particular operations. But they know far less than the library does (if, in fact, they know anything at all) about what the community's other institutions are up to. As Cindi Hickey, a library technology consultant, points out, "Libraries are our local nodes for information. Since they are already tied into the community, local libraries are uniquely positioned to adapt information to the particular needs of the community."[2]

Community networking is not about going it alone. Quite the contrary. It is about pulling together many different institutions, individuals, and constituencies. Community networking motivates institutions to develop a more external focus: to move beyond the four walls of the institution and be further integrated into the community. By cooperating and partnering with other institutions in the community, libraries spread the risk and the effort. As a result, the library and its community networking partners deliver a product of far greater value to the community and its citizens.

Although the mix of local institutions that collaborate to develop the community network varies from community to community, typical partners include:

- Library
- School
- College or university
- Government (municipal, county, regional, state, federal)
- Nonprofit agencies
- Telephone company or other utility
- Media organization (newspaper, cable, television or radio station)
- Hospital
- Business
- Economic development agencies: chamber of commerce, bureau of tourism[3]

As you looked over this list, did you notice how the institutions in the community have overlapping constituencies? For instance, library patrons also need health care and wellness information. Property owners have children in the public school. University professors support the public library. The list goes on and on. The point is that your "customers" are their customers. You will get more support and enthusiasm if you are seen as reaching out, cooperating to deliver an important public service.

Librarians should be willing to initiate the effort: to seek out others in the community who can be persuaded to share your vision for the future and the importance of online information services. As Susan Holmes, director of the Three Rivers Free-Net in Pittsburgh, says, "Libraries offer neutral mission statements, neutral sites, neutral content, and a dedication to presenting all points of view. [Community networking] is a natural extension of the library's community outreach program."[4] Your efforts to band together your community's institutions should strike a responsive chord. After all, what community institution is not interested in preserving—enhancing—the health, the well-being, the very existence of the community? Who does not want to see the community prosper and grow or, at the very least, not wither and die? What community institution does not have an important stake in the future of the community?

So, why should librarians participate in community networks? In short, because you have to—that is, if you want to ensure the long-run future of your institution. But, remember, you are not alone: the other institutions in your community are in a similar state. Everyone is faced with figuring out how to be more proactive and externally focused, how to reach out and be more integrated into the lifeblood of the community. This can be a powerful basis for collaboration: everyone puts in something but gets a lot in return.

Even though there is a great deal of public support generally for libraries, their long-run future has been questioned by some. Consider the following comment from a publication of the Benton Foundation:

> Americans continue to have a love affair with their libraries, but they have difficulty figuring out where libraries fit in the new digital world. And many Americans would just as soon turn their local libraries into museums and recruit retirees to staff them. Libraries are thus at a crossroads, for they must adjust their traditional values and services to the digital age. But there is good reason for optimism as libraries and their communities take up this challenge. Libraries have enormous opportunities nationwide to influence and direct public opinion because strong public sentiment already supports key visions for the future of libraries. Moreover, the growing use of home computers seems, at least at this juncture, to complement—not compete with—library use. So libraries and their leaders now must chart a role for themselves, giving meaning and message to their future institutions and their central role in community life.[5]

Community Networking Services

There is a continuum of services that community networks can provide, including

- Local information database
- Public access
- Training, support, and technical assistance
- Electronic mail
- Interactive group communications

- Dial-up access
- Administration
- Volunteer management
- Membership management

At one end of the services continuum, the community network is virtual: it exists entirely online, in "cyberspace," requiring only space on an Internet-accessible computer (a Web server) and minimal Web page creation and maintenance activities. At the other end of the continuum, the community network is not only virtual and online but it maintains a "real world" presence in the community: it is an established nonprofit organization with physical facilities, an extensive technology infrastructure, staff and volunteers, and members who "belong." Where you place your community network along this continuum depends upon the level of need for community networking services, interest and enthusiasm in the community for having and using these services, and the level of resources committed to delivering these services.

Below is an overview of each of these potential community networking services.[6]

Local Information Database

Creating local information databases involves developing and maintaining local electronic information resources. This is the primary focus for most community networks and the reason most community networks are first established. Once community information is developed, it must be stored and made accessible online. This is done by means of a file server—basically a computer with specialized software and a very large storage capacity. A simple community network, which can be set up as a part of another server, merely serves as the "virtual community square," a directory providing hyperlinks to all existing Web pages that relate to the community in some way. However, a true community network actively solicits information to deliver online and offers its own database of information that is not available online from other sources.

Providing online space is relatively easy these days—the success of the network concept rests largely with recruiting local information providers who can and will provide timely, accurate information that affects, assists, and informs the members of the community.

The community network decides who can be an information provider, consistent with the policies, goals, and resources of the organization. Typically, public-sector and nonprofit information providers such as libraries; local, regional, and state government; schools; hospitals; religious, civic, and community organizations; and social service agencies are considered key sources of information. Businesses and economic development groups can also provide valuable public information.

Every community has a unique set of potential information providers that can be identified and developed. A wide range of information providers best serves the community, and the community network should strongly encourage all appropriate agencies and organizations to participate. Therefore, this function can be expanded to include advertising, marketing, and public relations activities to get the word out about the services offered to potential information providers.

Keep in mind that the information provider is donating this information in the interest of the community. Accordingly, the community network needs to develop clear and easy-to-use methods that make it efficient and user-friendly for the information provider to submit, revise, and delete information. Simplifying this process encourages the information providers to maintain high-quality sites and ensures that the end user has access to timely, accurate information.

The information providers must in turn be willing to accept the responsibility and challenge of providing current, valuable information to the community, to support the community network, and to remain committed to this process. Information providers may need to register in order to participate and should have a clear understanding of what constitutes information acceptable to the community network. Information providers should have a great sense of pride in participating in the community network and contributing this public service. Information providers should also encourage other agencies to join and support the community network.

Since the community network will often be run with a number of volunteers or personnel with multiple duties, and may be operating with limited resources for at least the first several years of operation, both information providers and community network staff need to minimize the time spent maintaining the local information base. Training programs, design templates, and at least semi-automated software functions and system administration support should be developed to help all parties involved develop and maintain the local information database without undue effort.

The local information database, once developed and stored, must be accessible to the community. Over the past few years, the Internet has become the most popular access method for community networks. The Internet is a worldwide "network of networks"—a global information system that links users together through computers. The actual operation of the Internet is a complex and highly technical undertaking, but using the Internet is a reasonably straightforward task for the end user. Internet access can be obtained through a variety of public- and private-sector Internet service providers (ISPs). Generally, users reach their Internet access point through dial-up (modem) access service over a regular telephone line or through some type of dedicated computer network connection.

Public Access

Public workstations give access to community information to citizens who do not have their own Internet-accessible computers or who are away from home or the office. Public access computer workstations can be located in libraries, town halls, or other public buildings; schools; churches; community centers; or even laundromats, grocery stores, and shopping malls. These workstations may provide Internet access through dial-up or network services.

Public access workstations are important as an explicit recognition that not all citizens in a community have access to a computer and modem. Public workstations allow all citizens to have access to information that might otherwise be unavailable.

Public access workstation users may have a variety of information access needs, but one of the most important needs is workstation accessibility during extended hours. Regardless of a person's daily schedule or an information provider's operating schedule, the community network can provide access to information and online services twenty-four hours a day. Accordingly, public access workstations need to be accessible to accommodate diverse personal schedules and information needs.

Training, Support, and Technical Assistance

A community network can also provide ongoing training, support, and technical assistance to its users and information providers. Many users need assistance to learn how to use the community network resources to their best advantage. New computer users may need very

basic training on how to start and use programs, while more experienced users may wish to learn more sophisticated information searching methods. The training program(s) can assist these users to get the
best possible use out of the network's resources. Most users will occa-
sionally run into a problem and will turn to the community network
for support and technical assistance. The same service needs also
apply to the network's information provider organizations—with the
added responsibility that they need to know how to deliver as well as
consume local information.

Electronic Mail

Providing e-mail capabilities to community network users requires
that an additional server computer be configured to operate the
e-mail system and store subscribers' e-mail messages. While providing
e-mail ensures that everyone in the community has access to e-mail,
there are now services available over the Internet that provide this service free of charge (if users will endure a bit of advertising). Whether
provided directly by the community network or not, e-mail capability enables individuals and organizations to interact electronically
with other subscribers. E-mail ensures that everyone on the network
has a voice, which promotes online discussion and offers an easy way
to solicit valuable input. This can be useful in building bonds between
users. Ensuring that information providers have e-mail capability
makes it possible for them to receive feedback from consumers about
the information they provide, resulting in added incentive to make
their information useful and timely.

Interactive Group Communications

One of the greatest benefits of online communication—and that
which sets it apart from other media—is its ability to foster two-way,
interactive communications between groups—small or large. To do
so, the community network provides a discussion list, bulletin board,
and/or "chat" capabilities on its file server or on an additional server
dedicated to these functions. Discussion lists and bulletin boards, like
e-mail, are "store and forward" technologies: messages are sent and
received at the convenience of users. Chat, on the other hand, occurs
in "real time." Participants must be online at the time the chat session
is occurring.

Electronic discussion lists can be used to stimulate group discussion and facilitate consensus. These lists rely on software that automates the sending and receiving of e-mail messages among relatively large groups of people. They are a good way to promote information-sharing and topical discussions among the community network's users. Discussion lists can be general or topic-specific and work similarly to magazine or newspaper subscriptions. That is, everyone who wants to be a part of the discussion subscribes to the list and receives copies of every message sent electronically to the list in his or her e-mail box. So, in order to be a part of these lists, each subscriber has to have e-mail capabilities. Discussion list messages can be stored and archived for future reference.

A useful service is to offer discussion list capability to the organizations that participate in the community network as a way for them to facilitate internal information-sharing and discussion.

Electronic bulletin boards offer another method for the community network to facilitate information-sharing and discussion among its users. Unlike discussion lists, users do not subscribe but use special computer software to view messages posted on electronic bulletin boards. Users can leave their own notices on the bulletin boards and respond to notices posted by others. Typical community network bulletin board topics include computer help desk, local issues forums, classified advertisements, and help wanted notices.

Chat, as the name implies, allows computer users to communicate with each other in real time. Chat is just like using a telephone—except you type instead of speak. While much has been made of the negative uses of chat, this capability can be offered selectively by the community network to enable convenient, large-group discussions on topics of local interest or importance.

Dial-up Access

Dial-up access allows citizens with a computer and modem to access community information from home, work, or school. While providing this service was a critical function for most community networks until the last year or two, most communities now are served by commercial ISPs that charge a monthly fee for Internet access. Community networks that provide this access usually do so free or at low cost to the users even though it may be a labor-intensive activity.

Administration

Administration of the community network is an ongoing activity that begins with the first organizational meeting and continues throughout the life of the network. The level of administration required will depend on (1) whether the community network is operated as a separate organization or as a component of one of its sponsors, (2) whether individuals and/or organizations actually belong—are members—or not, and (3) the offered number and sophistication of the online services.

Proper community network administration makes using the network much more effective for the user and makes sustainability of the network more likely. The technical administrative function performed by the community network can consist of preventive maintenance, disk backups, usage monitoring, system upgrades, and other services to keep the underlying computer and telecommunications systems running smoothly.

Volunteer Management

Community networks frequently develop a corps of dedicated, trained volunteers to enable the delivery of cost-effective services. Volunteers also help to ensure the long-run sustainability of the community network. While volunteers can be vital to the overall success of the community network, effective volunteer management is essential.

Membership Management

The community network can exist as a distinct, community-based organization to which members—individuals and organizations— belong. In general, community networks that have members require an annual, paper-based renewal process—this provides an ongoing opportunity to solicit and to receive donations. In addition to a ready source of revenue generation, members offer the community network the potential of a loyal cadre of supporters and an ongoing "customer base." In order to realize this potential, the community network needs to establish a workable system that can support the membership and that delivers high-quality customer service.

New Possibilities

If you share this belief that the Information Age is real and that online information is an important part of everyone's future, you should be willing to redeploy some of your organization's current resources toward community networking. Many organizations will say, "Give us the money and we'll be glad to provide that service." But isn't that turf-building? I am not saying you cannot look for creative funding to subsidize your community networking efforts. But if you think it is important enough to the future of your organization and to your community, you need to reevaluate your priority list and figure out how to make it happen.

At its core, a community network is an information system. Information systems come in two varieties: operational and strategic. Operational information systems are designed to increase productivity and efficiency and reduce the costs associated with performing existing activities. On the other hand, strategic information systems are designed to enable new ways of doing things. While operational information systems are certainly important, focusing solely on operational outcomes limits one's ability to see information as a strategic resource. Similarly, focusing solely on the operational aspects often condemns the information system to be viewed as a cost to be contained rather than as an investment to be exploited to its full potential.

Sure it's nice to save time and money—that's what operational information systems do. But wouldn't it be nicer to facilitate community interaction in whole new ways—ways that were not possible before the invention of these technologies—all the while saving time and money, too? If so, think how community networking can enable you to aim high, to exploit this technology, to invest in the community, to deliver innovative information services in whole new ways. I would venture to say no one knows more about this stuff than you do. No one is better equipped to get informed than you. And the time to think about it is now. Otherwise, someone else might define your role—or worse, leave you out entirely.

What new information products and services can you envision? While providing online space for local organizations is important and a good way to start, aim to innovate constantly and deliver services that people really need and want—information services that will positively affect people's daily lives. You know the kinds of information library patrons typically request. You know the kinds of questions they need answers to. Make this a focus for your community networking efforts: to proactively meet the information needs of your community.

Think of the advantages of online information sources in relation to other publication media such as print or CD-ROM. For instance, online information is easily updated. Therefore, it is easier to keep current. Not easy—just easier. While you cannot reprint a book every-day or cut a new CD, you can change a Web page. What can online technology do that other media (print, radio, television) cannot? Online systems allow full, two-way, interactive communications from one to one, one to many, many to one, and many to many. How can you exploit this technology to enable citizen interaction in whole new ways? For instance:

> How might the community network's fully interactive technology be exploited so that the nonprofit human services agencies can share information within and between one another to meet the critical needs of the community and avoid duplication of effort?

> How might the community network facilitate citizen access to government information currently hidden deep within government databases? What could be done to make it easier for citizens to get data from multiple, separate government agencies simultaneously?

> How might the community network facilitate communication between neighborhood watch groups and the community policing units in order to reduce crime and improve safety?

Another point to keep in mind: technology is just a means to an end. Your real goals are to improve your community and to ensure the long-run viability of the community (and, by extension, your institution's vital place in the community). As an information professional, you plan to meet these goals by delivering online information services. The point may seem subtle but it really is not. If you keep your end goals in mind, you will ensure that your community networking initiatives improve your community in high-priority, positive ways.

The Synergy between Libraries and Community Networks

Joan Durrance, a professor in the School of Information at the University of Michigan and a long-time community networking advocate, suggests there are many similarities between libraries and community networks. For instance:

No one is required to use the library or the community network; people use them voluntarily

Both have as a major goal to increase citizens' access to information

Both seek to improve the quality of life in community

Both have grassroots beginnings

Both focus on meeting the information needs of the community

Both staunchly defend freedom of information and oppose censorship

Both recognize the importance of local content as part of their collections

Both require strong community support to succeed

Both sense some competition

Both engage in collaboration

Both good libraries and good community networks have an impact in their community

On the other hand, there are differences between libraries and community networks:

Age—public libraries have existed for a century; community networks for a decade

Service scope—libraries treat online sources as an additional information medium; community networks deal solely with online information

Type of presence—libraries maintain a physical presence in the community; the community network's presence is more often virtual

Gender use—heavy users of the library tend to be educated women; until recently, far more men were online

Funding patterns—there is a great deal of public support for library funding; the long-run sustainability of community networks is uncertain

As a community institution, the library is unique and brings many benefits to a community network:

Wide-ranging community trust, understanding, and experience working in the community

Planning experience

Marketing and promotion of the community network

Potential for sustained funding

As a physical place in the community, the library can provide space for the community networking headquarters, equipment, and physical meetings; offer public access computer terminals; provide community networking training services; and provide the physical, public space where citizens can "connect" with the community network.

Along with schools, libraries are one of the primary "public spaces" where people in the community can congregate. Since they are often miles ahead of other public institutions in terms of their technological experience and knowledge, it makes sense for libraries to play a key role in organizing community networks.

Apart from the library as an institution, librarians themselves possess critical skills and experience needed by the community network:

Ability to organize and catalog information for easy retrieval

Professional commitment to universal access and intellectual freedom

Skills in helping people to find what they need and to learn new technologies

A sense of community needs

Skills in volunteer management

Expertise in policy development

Experience with collaboration

Librarians are professionals trained to identify, organize, and provide access to information, which makes them perfect navigators for communities trying to make sense and use of a global network of information. "[T]raining librarians to become both skilled cyberspace navigators and digital resource publishers is a prerequisite for the development of a successful Web-based community network." [7] On the other hand, librarians also have strong feelings on issues such as filtering and censorship—issues that the community network may need to address.

If you are worried that you and your community are "behind the eight ball" in terms of community networking, don't be. Keep in mind that new technologies take a long time to reach critical mass—that point in time when it seems the once-new technology is everywhere and everyone is using it. For instance, cable TV and the Internet have each been around for more than twenty-five years. Cellular phones have existed for a decade. The microwave oven, the VCR, and the fax machine, some of the most successful consumer products in history, are based on technologies that had been around for a long time before their use took off. It takes the right combination of factors for a new technology to reach critical mass. A product must be available at the right price and be easy to use before customer demand will take off. Therefore, this is actually a very good time to become involved with community networking. Everyone is trying to figure out how to make it all come together and provide useful, beneficial services. Shouldn't you be part of this effort?

Next Steps

At this point I hope that you are convinced that community networking is an important strategy to meet your community's electronic information services needs and that you are excited enough to consider getting yourself and your organization involved. At this point, you may want to read more about what constitutes community networking and why it is so important. Or you may want to go online to "visit" some community networks or to gather resource materials to adapt for your own community. You have many options. Just don't choose to do nothing. Your community, your library, and you personally cannot afford that!

Wherever you go from here, keep in mind the advice I heard over and over again from those I interviewed: Just do it! To that I will add my own personal two cents worth: Have fun! Be enthusiastic about the possibilities. Craft a situation that excites you. Work with people you like and admire. Then be an advocate for equitable access to information resources and services throughout your community. Do what you can to make cyberspace a better place to be. Be an information resource to others. I hope this book lends you a helping hand.

Remember that each community is unique and so is its community network. If a network is already established or planned for your community, consider what you and your organization can do to become involved. Learn about the organizational structure. Inquire what service areas need the most assistance. Determine if a critical service has yet to be implemented. Think, too, about your level of commitment. How much time do you have available? What current duties will you need to let slide? How much money or in-kind contributions could your organization redeploy?

If no efforts are currently underway, consider how to start. Begin by thinking what your organization could put in: People? Space? Money? Equipment? Expertise? Then consider what other community institutions might be interested in becoming involved.

If you are interested in going beyond the community networking field for ideas and inspiration, I recommend you examine literature in the areas of (1) information and referral and (2) community organizing and development. Information and referral, commonly referred to as I&R, is a service that began in the 1970s to help people in need of human services find the agency or individual that could best serve that need. The task of delivering I&R services in local communities, if they are available, usually falls to the United Way, the public library, a government office, or an independent I&R agency. I&R professionals have spent the past twenty years figuring out the best ways to catalog local human service agencies and now need to work on "self-service" methods of information access. Since I&R-type services usually represent an important component of most local community networks, I recommend you pursue a strategy of mutual support and cooperation with your local I&R agency if one exists. Additional information about I&R is contained in chapter 8.

The community organizing and development literature promotes a proactive, grassroots approach to community problem solving by working to get average citizens involved in public life. This field, which developed largely out of the protest marches of the 1960s, has evolved considerably since then. Combing this literature will offer you many down-to-earth tips about how to frame your issues, build coalitions of support, and achieve your objectives.

In particular, I recommend Mark Homan's *Promoting Community Change*. This book takes a hands-on, practical look at the process of change and offers useful techniques for bringing about change effectively—regardless of the setting. Although his message is aimed primarily at social work graduate students and other human services professionals, I very much enjoy the style Homan takes in this book. His ideas echo those my parents taught me a long time ago: that a professional—someone with years and years of education who relies more on brains than brawn—works to earn the right to pass on to others what he or she has learned. Moreover a professional has the responsibility to share this knowledge in order to make the world a better place for everyone. As Homan states:

> You cannot take sole responsibility for the problems you see, nor can you tackle them all. You do, however, need to make a conscious decision to help change policies and improve conditions whose limitations contribute to problems people in your community experience. It is important that you acknowledge this as a legitimate, if not fundamental, part of your role as a . . . professional.[8]

Community Networking Organizations

The Association for Community Networking (AFCN) (bcn.boulder.co.us/afcn/), formally established in 1998, plans to be the primary membership organization for those interested in community networking. AFCN hopes to improve the visibility, viability, and vitality of community networking. AFCN objectives are to assist and connect people and organizations, build public awareness about community networking, identify and share best practices, encourage research, influence policy, and develop products and services. AFCN plans to examine the range of collaborating partners involved at the local level in community networking projects and plans to bring them together at the national level. These activities are designed to support, enhance, and stimulate the kinds of collaborations we would like to be taking place at the local level. Start-up funding was provided by the Morino Institute, Apple Computer, University of Michigan School of Information, and the W. K. Kellogg Foundation. Ongoing funding is to be provided by dues-paying members, services and products, and grants. Membership (currently $75 for individuals residing in the United

States and a sliding scale for organizations) entitles you to the bimonthly print newsletter, mailing lists, Web presence, discounts on AFCN products and services (such as conferences and publications), a vote for the board of directors, and eligibility to serve on the board of directors.

The Center for Civic Networking (www.civicnet.org) promotes best practices and policies that foster the public use of information infrastructure for community economic development, social service delivery, and participation in governance. This mission is pursued through research, education, consulting, and special project activities. The center teams with civic, nonprofit, small business, and government organizations to develop and promote information infrastructure applications that can sustain healthy communities. The center, a not-for-profit organization based in Massachusetts, was founded in 1993.

Community Technology Centers' Network (CTCNet) (www.ctcnet. org) brings together agencies and programs that provide opportunities whereby people of all ages who typically lack access to computers and related technologies can learn to use these technologies in an environment that encourages exploration and discovery and, through this experience, develop personal skills and self-confidence. Further details about this organization and its projects are contained in chapter 9.

Organization for Community Networks (www.ofcn.org) is an Ohio-based nonprofit established as a central repository for information dealing with Free-Nets and Community Networks. As a follow-up to the former NPTN, this site contains documents that have been supplied by various systems to share with new and existing systems. Includes community network document libraries, conferences and special interest items, current legislation affecting community networks, medical center, academy center, teledemocracy center, resource center, and a "teleolympics."

For More Information

Communet: The Community and Civic Network Discussion List. (communet@uvm.edu)

This electronic discussion list provides persons interested in community networking with a forum to discuss broad information policy issues as well as day-to-day operational issues and currently serves as the primary means of information sharing for persons in the community networking field. To subscribe send the following message to listserv@list.uvm.edu:

> subscribe communet yourfirstname yourlastname.

(For a searchable, comprehensive list of electronic discussion lists, contact Liszt, the Mailing List Directory, at www.liszt.com/)

Community Computer Networks and Web Sites. (www.victoria.tc.ca/freenets.html)

Maintained by volunteers of the Victoria, British Columbia, Telecommunity Network. Organized by country, this site is quite comprehensive and provides hyperlinks to community networks that provide interactive access. Also includes links to community networking organizations, conferences, and related materials. This is an excellent "first stop" if you want to learn where community networking initiatives are underway or if you want to connect to a particular community network and are unsure of its URL.

Community Networking Initiative. (www.si.umich.edu/Community/)

This research project at the University of Michigan School of Information is spearheaded by Dr. Joan Durrance, a professor and long-time advocate of community networking, and supported by the W. K. Kellogg Foundation. This site provides a wealth of information about existing community networks as well as resources for any community wishing to get one established. Resources include:

The Work of Community Networks: Directory, Community Networking Showcase, Community Partnerships, What's New?

The Resource Center: Community Information, Reading Room, Funding, Technology, Discussion/Conferences

Connections: A Journal of Current Events in Community Networking

Community Networking Movement. (www.scn.org/ip/commnet/)

This Web site, maintained by Doug Schuler, a longtime community networking advocate and author of *New Community*

Networks: Wired for Change, provides information and resources about community networking.

Community Networking Partnerships.
(www.libsci.sc.edu/stephen/CNResearch.htm)

This Web site, which I maintain, tracks and categorizes the partnership arrangements established by community networks in the United States and Canada. Here you can inquire, for instance, how many and which community networks consider the library to be a major partner.

Community Networks: Lessons from Blacksburg, Virginia, edited by Andrew Michael Cohill and Andrea L. Kavanaugh. Norwood, Mass.: Artech House, 1997. ISBN: 0890068968.

Computer Donations to Schools: A Review of Selected Private-Sector, Nonprofit, and State Programs, by Walter S. Baer and Gwendolyn Farnsworth. 1997.   (www.rand.org/publications/DB/DB222/)

Cyberdemocracy: Technology, Cities and Civic Networks, edited by Roza Tsagarousianou, Damian Tambini, and Cathy Bryan. New York: Routledge, 1998. Hard cover ISBN: 0415171342. Paperback ISBN: 0415171350.

"Developing the Blacksburg Electronic Village," by John M. Carroll and Mary Beth Rosson. *Communications of the ACM* 39, no.12 (December 1996): 69–75.

Local Places, Global Connections: Libraries in the Digital Age, by Libraries for the Future (LFF) and the Benton Foundation. Washington, D.C.: Benton Foundation, 1997.

This report reflects a conviction that libraries are uniquely suited to make the benefits of new information technologies available to everyone, regardless of economic status or place of residence. Further details about this report are contained in chapter 9.

New Community Networks: Wired for Change, by Douglas Schuler. Reading, Mass.: Addison-Wesley, 1996. ISBN: 0201595532.

This was the first book specifically about community networking to be published. This wise and informative book explains how grassroots networks can be implemented at little cost in a socially directed way. As a founding member of the Seattle Community Network—one of the first and most innovative free networking projects in the world—Schuler provides great practical advice with a refreshing dose of social conscience.

Surplus Federal Computers for Schools: An Assessment of the Early Implementation of Executive Order 12999, by Thomas K. Glennan, Jr., Walter S. Baer, Susanna Purnell, Gwendolyn Farnsworth, and Gina Schuyler. 1997. (www.rand.org/publications/MR/MR871/)

Smart Communities. (www.smartcommunities.org)

This Web site is one component of a joint project between the California State Department of Transportation (Caltrans) and the International Center for Communications at San Diego State University. The "smart community" concept says that local leaders know far better than state or national officials how next-generation technologies can best be marshaled to a community's benefit. It says that only local political, civic, business, and education leaders, working in cooperation, can bring people and technology together in time to capture the competitive and civic advantages that the telecommunications revolution makes possible. Included at this Web site are a guidebook and implementation materials for communities interested in the smart communities concept as well as case studies of communities nationwide that have evolved into "smart communities."

Universal Access to E-Mail: Feasibility and Societal Implications, by Robert H. Anderson, Tora K. Bikson, Sally Ann Law, and Bridger M. Mitchell. 1995. (www.rand.org/publications/MR/MR650/)

NOTES

1. *The Change Masters,* by Rosabeth Moss Kanter (New York: Simon & Schuster, 1983).
2. *Local Places, Global Connections: Libraries in the Digital Age,* by Libraries for the Future (LFF) and the Benton Foundation (Washington, D.C.: Benton Foundation, 1997). Used with permission. Copies are available from the Benton Foundation (www.benton.org), 1634 Eye Street, NW, Washington, DC 20006, phone: 202/638-5770 or from Libraries for the Future (LFF) (www.lff.org), 121 W. 27th Street, Suite 1102, New York, NY 10001; phone: 212/352-2330, fax: 212/352-2342.
3. For more information about the partnership arrangements of the established community networks, see the "Community Networking Research" section I maintain on my Web site. (www.libsci.sc.edu/stephen/bajjaly.htm)
4. Susan Holmes, communication to the author.

5. *Buildings, Books, and Bytes: Libraries and Communities in the Digital Age.* (www. benton.org/Library/Kellogg/home.html)
6. Material in this section has been adapted from the Missouri Express Web site (outreach.missouri.edu/moexpress/) and from "Moving from an Access Site to a Community Net," by David Murdoch, Chebucto Community Network, Halifax, Nova Scotia. Used with permission.
7. *Local Places, Global Connections,* p. 24.
8. *Promoting Community Change: Making It Happen in the Real World,* by Mark S. Homan (Pacific Grove, Calif.: Brooks/Cole, 1994).

Planning the Community Network

So you think that community networking makes sense for your community. It fits within the mission of your library or other community-based organization. You and a small group of others who share your enthusiasm are willing to "take the plunge" and work to establish your own local community network. This chapter addresses perhaps the most important task you can undertake in community networking: initiating the process.

Being a part of a community network from the beginning enables you to create an organization that will share your vision of how electronic information services should be delivered in your community in the years ahead. Even if your community already has a community network but your library or organization is not an active partner, this chapter will provide you with ideas to consider.

Setting a Direction

Setting a direction for your community network by articulating its principles, purpose, and vision are critical to getting your community network off to a solid start.[1] The success of your community network—that it meets the needs of the community—is dependent upon forming a shared sense of purpose and vision for the project. A community network is, after all, run by the community for the community.

Community network organizers who have struggled with sustaining partners' participation, user services, information providers, and sufficient funding repeatedly point out that the problems were often rooted in the failure to take sufficient time and devote sufficient attention up front to developing a clear sense of shared direction, collective ownership, and responsibility.

Therefore, setting a direction represents the single most important task, and it must be accomplished before anything else. As the network's initial leader, heading this "visioning process" is your reward for starting efforts in the first place. These early actions will set the direction for the later planning process and the future of the network. And they will serve as important criteria for measuring the usefulness of ideas, strategies, and initiatives at any stage of the network's development or operation.

To obtain a clearer sense of a community network's direction, you could examine various networks' Web sites. For instance, the mission statement for the Austin Free-Net (www.austinfree.net) in Austin, Texas, is clearly articulated on its home page:

> The primary mission of the Austin Free-Net (AFN) is to provide public access to the Internet and emerging technologies for all Austin residents, especially those who don't have computers in their homes.

Notice how the AFN mission does not say anything about providing information—it leaves those aspects of community networking to other groups. The AFN works in close collaboration with the Austin Public Library to provide public access to technology as well as the needed training, support, and technical assistance. Overall, the AFN is a cooperative effort involving Austin educational, civic, and corporate entities. Other participating organizations include the University of Texas, Literacy Austin, Austin Learning Academy, City of Austin Police and Fire departments, Austin Independent School District, and other community organizations, private companies, and communications providers. Elsewhere on the AFN Web site you will find more details about its vision, goals, and objectives:

> **AFN Vision:** Use the Internet and other emerging technologies to connect people with information, services and people.
>
> At its core, the AFN provides Internet-connected computers and training in public spaces for the greater benefit of all residents. In look-

ing at barriers to access to information, the AFN discovered that the main barriers in Austin are not related to connectivity costs but rather to equipment and training costs.

AFN Purpose: To provide every member of the Austin community access, through public access sites, to the Internet/National Information Infrastructure by the year 2000.

The AFN and its partners believe that businesses and people of Austin Texas want to be leaders in developing equitable access to the information superhighway and the Austin Free-Net is here to make that happen.

AFN focuses much of its attention on the needs of children and youth in low income families. By using the Internet, young people can touch the broad array of possibilities for their lives while connecting with critical educational and health services needed by their families.

Another purpose is clearly stated by the Ozarks Regional Information Online Network (ORION):

> The mission of ORION is to develop and maintain a regional electronic network which will provide access to local, national, and international information sources for residents of Springfield and the Southwest Missouri region.

Southeast Florida Library Information Network (SEFLIN) is a nonprofit membership organization of Southeast Florida libraries that was founded in the late 1980s with LSCA federal grant funds. SEFLIN strives to pioneer innovative technology to deliver optimum library services to South Florida. SEFLIN operates the SEFLIN Free-Net as an extension of its primary mission:

> SEFLIN believes that libraries can make a difference in people's lives. Our mission is to work cooperatively with our members and the community to promote the collection and sharing of library resources, to facilitate training, to increase public awareness, to provide leadership, to encourage the joint use of technology, and to support activities that enhance an individual library's ability to meet the informational, educational, and cultural needs of its primary users and Southeast Florida residents. SEFLIN will position SEFLIN libraries as major leaders in the information structure of Southeast Florida by working cooperatively with libraries, educational institutions, information agencies, area business, and government agencies.
>
> SEFLIN will enable libraries to transcend political boundaries and empower people to receive the information they need when they need it. SEFLIN libraries will affirm the social value of libraries as key

contributors to the community's social and economic well-being and quality of life.

SEFLIN libraries will facilitate the joint use of technology to provide residents of Southeast Florida with links to local, state, regional, and global information resources.

The Seattle Community Network, one of the oldest community networks in existence, clearly articulates its mission and its commitments:

The Seattle Community Network (SCN) is a free public-access computer network for exchanging and accessing information. Beyond that, however, it is a service conceived for community empowerment. Our principles are a series of commitments to help guide the ongoing development and management of the system for both the organizers and participating individuals and organizations.

Commitment to Access: Access to the SCN will be free to all. We will provide access to all groups of people, particularly those without ready access to information technology. We will provide access to people with diverse needs. This may include special-purpose interfaces. We will make the SCN accessible from public places.

Commitment to Service: The SCN will offer reliable and responsive service. We will provide information that is timely and useful to the community. We will provide access to databases and other services.

Commitment to Democracy: The SCN will promote participation in government and public dialogue. The community will be actively involved in the ongoing development of the SCN. We will place high value on freedom of speech and expression and on the free exchange of ideas. We will make every effort to ensure privacy of the system users. We will support democratic use of electronic technology.

Commitment to the World Community: In addition to serving the local community, we will become part of the regional, national and international community. We will build a system that can serve as a model for other communities.

Commitment to the Future: We will continue to evolve and improve the SCN. We will explore the use of innovative applications such as electronic town halls for community governance, or electronic encyclopedias for enhanced access to information. We will work with information providers and with groups involved in similar projects using other media. We will solicit feedback on the technology as it is used, and make it as accessible and humane as possible.

The commonality among these community networks is that each clearly sets a direction for the delivery of community networking services that responds to the needs of its particular community. While it is fine, and even desirable, to draw upon the work of other communities for inspiration, you should develop your own sense of direction that clearly responds to the particular needs of your community.

Forming a Steering Committee

After you have a clear sense of what you think your community network should "look like," you need to create an empowered steering committee representative of the important stakeholder groups and organizations in your community. Then you must ensure that the steering committee follows through on its charge to implement community networking services that focus on the community's most pressing electronic information needs.

Both of these tasks involve leadership and planning. At first you must take charge to develop an empowered steering committee. Then, this committee must

Develop a vision for community networking in your community

Conduct a thorough assessment of community needs and capabilities

Prepare a business plan to guide the development and operation of the community network

Chances are, you think of yourself as a team player: willing to do whatever you're asked to do, anxious to do a good job. But you don't want to be in charge, to get a group together, to assign the tasks. If this sounds like you, then your thoughts echo the overwhelming majority of community networking organizers I interviewed for this book. These are people who think of themselves as enthusiastic, capable, and quality-oriented; uncomfortably thrust into the spotlight to evangelize the cause of community networking. Fortunately, every one of these nervous leaders found the project to be worth the effort and the initial trepidation.

There is a difference between management and leadership. Management is a science, whereas leadership is closer to an art. Management is about the *how* of doing things, whereas leadership is subtler and has to do with the *why*. . . . One cannot be even a passable leader without management competence. But management without the extra attribute of leadership can be a hollow thing. Management *manages;* it lets things happen. Leadership *leads;* it initiates and makes things happen.[2]

Most of my interviewees indicated that their initial steering committees included approximately ten members. This seems to be an effective working size: not so large that the decision-making process is cumbersome and not so small that important issues will be overlooked. Some thoughts to consider:

Be sure this committee generally represents all segments of the community.

Try for technology champions, not "techies." Remember the technology is just your means to an end. You want people who strongly believe in this concept as a means to improve the community. Too many techies and the system may be a technological wonder but useless to most members of the community.

Think about your own organization first. What skills, attitudes, and constituencies do you bring to the steering committee? Then try to find community representatives to complement what you offer.

As noted in chapter 2, some of the organizations to consider when developing the steering committee include libraries (your own and others), school district, local government, health care providers, nonprofit organizations and consortia such as the United Way, phone companies, ISPs, utilities, and business organizations such as chambers of commerce and bureaus of economic development or tourism.

You need to be sure that you create an empowered steering committee. That is, you want a steering committee that has the power and the capability to make decisions that will be implemented. This committee should be action oriented; include at least some influential, experienced decision makers; and be directly responsible for budget development and oversight.

While every community is unique and the method of community network development can vary widely, there are four critical success factors to keep in mind. The presence of these factors does not guarantee success—nor does their absence doom you to fail—but they are generally present in the successful, sustainable networks. These factors are

Technology champions—Involve organizational leaders who believe strongly in the concept of community networking and who have sufficient power and influence within their respective organizations and the community as a whole to commit the necessary resources to get the project up and running. Typical community networking champions include library directors, local government managers, university computer services managers.

Broad community support—A community network is run by the community for the community. Since it takes considerable time, money, and effort to sustain the network over the long run, in order for the project to be worthwhile the community needs to support the network and use its services.

Deep-pocketed partners—Most communities, even if they receive some seed-money grants, take a risk in establishing a community network. It helps if the founding partners are large, well-funded institutions that can afford to "ante up" the necessary funding to get the network off the ground and sustain it at least until it becomes established.

Volunteer management—Developing a strong corps of committed volunteers not only helps to ensure the long-run sustainability of the community network but also provides the necessary trained personnel to enable the delivery of cost-effective services.

Citizens and Consumers

Mary Virnoche, Research and Evaluation Coordinator for the Boulder Community Network, suggests that decisions that shape the visions of community networks are influenced by two social currents or sentiments: civic and consumer.[3]

A democratic idealism underscores the civic orientation. There is a desire to bring Internet-based technologies to those least able to secure access and participation on their own: the information "have nots." Also the principle, borrowed from the hacker culture, of the "ideal public sphere"—one that is unfettered by private or commercial influence—is important.

On the other hand, the cornerstone of the consumer orientation rests firmly in organizational stability, and the focus for community building is broadly defined. While nontraditional users may be a part of the discussion, a consumer orientation is more squarely focused on those who already support or are more easily enticed to use the technology. Although a consumer orientation is rife with pragmatic operational concerns, it often leads to interesting results, and creates enthusiasm in the private sector.

Civic and consumer sentiments do not operate in isolation. They may exist quietly or noticeably side by side. They can and sometimes do complement each other. Yet their incongruencies may surface and create tensions within and between community network organizers—especially at key decision points or contingencies.

Virnoche identifies four variables on which tension between the civic and the consumer sentiments can rest:

Information format—text-only or multimedia

Information content—solely nonprofit or includes business

Online interaction—whether the community network provides a one-way, downstream, broadcast model of information delivery or incorporates tools to permit users to interact and provide feedback

Outreach level—the extent to which the community network strives to get content from and make online access available to diverse groups within the community

While those with a civic orientation push text-only interfaces, exclusively nonprofit content, full electronic interaction capabilities for everyone, and deep outreach, those with a decided consumer orientation would favor graphical interfaces, including profit-making content, limited interaction options, and little to moderate outreach. The extent to which tension is experienced depends upon the points of view of the community network's principal designers.

Format, Content, and Audience

Until the invention of the Web in the mid-1990s, online computing required considerable technical knowledge. The Web has brought three important advances to the Internet and accounts for the vast popularity of online communications: multimedia access, hypertext links, and ease of use. Prior to the Web, the Internet was strictly text-based (letters and numbers). As a multimedia application, the Web permits Internet users to access data in all its forms: pictures (graphics), video (moving graphics), and sound.

While a text-only interface provides almost equal access to the important, substantial "stuff" on the Internet, a graphical interface can be more seductive with its flashy layout and point-and-click multimedia options. Yet navigating a text format is possible even with the oldest computer technology, whereas the graphical interface requires far more sophisticated technology. In particular, up-to-date computers provide faster online access via higher-speed modems, faster CPUs, and more RAM. So even within a population of people who have access to some type of computer, a "technogap" exists between those with computing technology ready to bring up a graphical interface and those with older technology limited to a text-only Internet.

Those who are computer savvy and financially secure are literally giving away their old computers and investing in newer models. Community networks are taking advantage of the swift technological and financial depreciation on computers and rerouting the discarded technology to organizations and agencies in need. Many people believe that some type of computer is better than none; nevertheless, hand-me-down computing practices set a pattern for the ongoing existence of some type of technogap.

Community networks, like any other group making information available on the Internet, make decisions about how to design that information. Designing for a text-based user is more consistent with a civic framework. Information designed to be read by a text-based interface is theoretically available to the greatest number of people. This accessibility is compatible with civic frameworks that equate community networking with broad-based grassroots initiative and use. On the other hand, many people just do not like text-based interfaces—especially once they have used a graphical interface. Regardless of preference, the text-based browser may be the only option for many nonprofit and human service agencies. Yet here we find a contradiction. Even though more people can theoretically play right now if they are willing to use text-based browsers, "real" use may not occur until graphical access is ubiquitous. Text-based design and browsing theoretically reach "deepest" into the populations. Yet people find them uninteresting and cumbersome to use. Graphics-based design and browsing have proven to be the attention grabbers. Yet the technology accompanying graphical browsers involves greater costs and set-up techniques.

One solution is to adopt a "dual formatting" approach whereby at least some information is accessible via text-based interfaces. This makes the information available to those with old computers and slow modems but still allows the community network to market itself to those people (and businesses) who want the glitz of the graphical interface. This same approach applies to frame-based Web pages. The drawback to this approach is that it is time-consuming and often tedious: system administrators must keep close track of Web page changes and ensure that the same changes are made to multimedia and text-only pages.

Unlike virtual communities, which can be magnets for dispersed homogeneous people or interests, community networks are positioned uniquely at a pivotal point because of their role of serving "geographic" communities that are likely to encompass competing interests of stratified heterogeneous community groups. This pivotal position has forced community network organizers to negotiate the dilemma of sustaining the greatest appeal of their networks (perhaps better served by the graphical interfaces) while adhering to the efforts to reach deep into the population and serve those with minimal technological capabilities (perhaps better served by text interfaces). They struggle with tempering their own elite skills, interests, and desires for "fun technologies" with providing information for everyone and access for everyone to their network. Agreeing that information will be designed for both worlds seems the most logical route. Yet with thousands of new Internet pages popping up every day, ensuring that community network information remains accessible to everyone is a very difficult task. There can be hundreds of people designing information pages for a single community network.

As community networks grow and involve more people, it may become more and more difficult to control information design to maintain broad, as well as deep-reaching, access. One cannot underestimate the seductive power of designing for "faster," "more colorful," and now "moving" information formats in a culture that is mesmerized by technology. Community members who volunteer their time to design network pages often enjoy the greater creative challenges of graphical design. And we must remember that even those with a strong civic information orientation are part of the technical elite who bubble with each new advance in design capabilities. When it comes down to it, designing for multimedia browsers is just more fun.

The above concerns overlap with another concern: defining who belongs to the community. Many community networks wrangle over whether to allow businesses and business-related information to cohabit on the community network. Those with a civic orientation often argue vehemently to exclude everything in any way related to commercialism. Discourse of those opposed to commercial information is often laden with idealism about community networking and lament of an Internet "gone bad" with commercialism. They maintain that any profit-making venture has no place on the community network. They are adamant that nonprofits be the only groups allowed to house their information on the community network's server.

On the other hand, those who argue for including profit-making information are often more concerned with sustaining and growing the community network than they are with adhering to an exclusively nonprofit service vision. These people are not only open to commercial ventures associating with the community network but believe some commercial aspect is crucial to survival.

At MidNet, we have focused on content rather than on who was ultimately providing the content. Like most community networks, we strictly prohibit advertising and we want the information we provide to be sufficiently general in nature to appeal to a broad spectrum of the community. But we welcome for-profit entities that have information to share with the general public. For instance, we have welcomed club listings from the area concert promoters, but we have encouraged state agencies to publish regulations that are of no interest or concern to the general public on government information servers.

Ten Rules of Community Network Success

As you think about how to proceed with community networking in the days, weeks, months, and years ahead, I would urge you to consider the remarks of Mario Morino, Chairman of the Morino Institute, which he made to an inaugural conference on community networking, Ties That Bind, hosted by Steve Cisler, a librarian and long-time community networking advocate, at Apple Computer headquarters in Cupertino, California, in 1994. Morino's comments—inspirational as they were at the time—I think have enduring value and suggest ideas to keep in mind when undertaking your own planning initiatives:

We would call upon community networks to reexamine their operations, to focus on lasting, positive social change, and to build networks as vehicles for community *action*. You have the opportunity to take years of hard-earned knowledge and experience and build a powerful new communications medium that can really help people change their lives. To that end, let us restate our ten suggestions toward ensuring the survival, the relevance, and the eventual prosperity of community networking:

1. Aim high: Work toward positive social change—set your vision on the ultimate goals of positive social change in your community, and maintain that focus in all that you do.

2. Serve the needs of community—build and develop your network to meet the ever-changing needs of your community.

3. Engage the broader community—expand and recompose your leadership to represent all the people you serve and establish an effective communications program within the community.

4. Broadly redefine support—establish an infrastructure, a support plan and full-time staff to support the community network.

5. Establish a sustaining economic model—move aggressively toward self-sufficiency and end dependence on outside funding.

6. Build a strong and open technological base—understand the issues of growth, scale, and interoperability—and how they relate to your system.

7. Make information relevant to your community—add value and context to the vast amounts of information available, by filtering and structuring it toward your local needs.

8. Ensure broad-based access—work to provide comprehensive physical access to your network, improve its ease of use, and make useful relevant knowledge a staple of its appeal.

9. Prepare for competitive times ahead—take an objective look at other not-for-profits, as well as commercial services, and look to strategic partnerships whenever possible.

10. Collaborate to represent a powerful movement—community networking leaders must reach out to one another, share information and resources, and speak to the world with a common voice—toward common goals.

The challenge we collectively face is: "How do we make community networking succeed by building on the formidable successes achieved by the pioneers of this new medium . . . to construct a grander, more encompassing, and higher vision?" A vision to support significant social action—of truly helping people change and improve their lives. We implore those of you "in the field" today to unite in this purpose and put aside philosophical differences. The grass-roots spirit and innovation that have fueled this explosion of talented, motivated, caring people is too big, too important, indeed, too crucial to our development as a people, to be stopped now.

You have a chance to affect history. The ramifications of what we do, how we grow the true concept and practice of community networking, will be felt for generations to come. We urge you to seize the opportunity, to make this next step, truly be a part of history. . . .[4]

Community Networking Models

I am often asked "Who are the role models for community networking?" This is a tough question to answer, since each community is unique and there are so many factors and circumstances that can "make or break" the success of a community network's initiatives. With these caveats in mind, there are several "good things" happening around the United States and Canada which I break down into broad initiatives and community initiatives.

Broad Initiatives

For the broad initiatives, there are two I know of that merit your attention: Missouri Express in the state of Missouri and the Community Access Program in Canada. These projects do what I think government should be doing relative to community networking: motivate communities within their jurisdictions to develop electronic information services; help these communities get started with local initiatives; keep communities from having to "reinvent the wheel" over and over by sharing information among and between local communities; and provide valuable services and technical assistance in an efficient, cost-effective manner. This is a totally appropriate role for your state library to play. Likewise, the state library can act as your primary link to state government and the state legislature to ensure that potential community networking initiatives receive the support and attention they deserve.

Missouri Express (outreach.missouri.edu/moexpress) was designed as a three-year capital improvements project with the goal of creating community information networks across the state of Missouri. A secondary purpose of the project is the development of electronic information resources for communities and citizens. It is intended that Missouri Express community networks must achieve sustainability by end of the project.

The concept for this project came from an initiative from the offices of Governor Mel Carnahan following discussions with the Missouri Office of Administration (OA) and the Missouri Research and Education Network (MOREnet). The Missouri General Assembly appropriated $6 million for state telecommunications services and the creation of up to eighty community information networks.

It is evident that a great deal of forethought and energy went into the development of the Missouri Express project. I am clearly impressed by the principles guiding the development of the Missouri Express project:

Fairness—All communities should be able to fully participate in the Information Age regardless of their current organizational or technological status. In the Missouri Express project, communities will have equal access to information, equipment, and support consistent with the needs of the community.

Simplicity—The success of the Missouri Express project depends on civic minded individuals and organizations who are willing to give their time to activities that benefit their community. Therefore, the Missouri Express project recognizes the need to make the development of community information networks as simple as possible. This principle will be incorporated in the application process, implementation phase, and in the provision of ongoing support to the community network.

Locally based decision making—Each community that chooses to be involved in the Missouri Express project has unique characteristics, values, and needs. Accordingly, each community will have the opportunity to determine its own organization, function, and content subject to legal and contractual restrictions. The key to the community information network's long-term success is its development as a valuable resource to the entire community.

Support to the communities—The Missouri Express project will provide locally based organizational assistance and technological support to any community requiring such support. Community information networks are at different levels of development across the state. Some communities will need considerable assistance to complete the project in a timely fashion, while other communities will require minimal support. The Missouri Express project partners will assist communities using support teams drawn from professionals based in the local area.

Results of the Missouri Express project are paying off for the residents of Missouri and beyond. This small state has more community networks (and more involvement of local public libraries) than any other. They have developed a wide range of useful resource materials: You will find references to many of Missouri Express's online resource guides throughout this book. Many community networking personnel across their state contributed to this book.

Industry Canada, the federal economic development agency, has instituted the "Community Access Project" (CAP) (cap.unb.ca) to help provide rural communities with affordable public access to the Internet as well as the skills to use it effectively. CAP is designed to create a national network of community access sites (CAP sites) to help create new and exciting opportunities for growth and jobs. Many of the public access projects profiled in chapter 9 received their start online with assistance from the Community Access Project.

CAP operates through a competitive process, whereby communities are chosen to establish and operate public access sites in low-cost public locations, such as schools and libraries, to serve as "Information highway on-ramps." Depending upon resource availability, the aim of CAP is to connect up to five thousand communities across Canada by 2001. Further information about CAP is available from its Web site or by phone (toll free in Canada only: 800-268-6608) or by e-mail: comaccess@ic.gc.ca

Community Initiatives

On a local or regional level, many community initiatives have caught my attention as I have researched this book. I am very excited by the work going on at the multitude of Missouri community networks spawned by the work of Missouri Express, as well as others I profile throughout this book. While it is often hard to judge how a particular community network is doing since so many factors come into play, this list represents some of the best community networking initiatives:

Austin Free-Net (www.austinfree.net/) in Austin, Texas, exemplifies a cooperative city government-library project to provide public access to technology in a very "high tech" city. AFN partners with many local organizations to ensure the community's online information needs are addressed.

Boulder Community Network (bcn.boulder.co.us/) in Boulder, Colorado, exemplifies a network that was established by academics at the University of Colorado to support ongoing research but has broadened to encompass the entire community.

Charlotte's Web (www.charweb.org/) in Charlotte, North Carolina, has broadened its base beyond Charlotte and Mecklenburg County to serve its entire region.

KooteNet (www.kootenet.net/) in Libby, Montana, exemplifies a public-private partnership to deliver online services in a very rural community.

SEFLIN Free-Net (www.seflin.org/) in Fort Lauderdale, Florida, exemplifies a system operated by a large library cooperative that is reaching out in innovative ways to serve an ethnically diverse community.

Tallahassee Free-Net (www.freenet.tlh.fl.us/) in Tallahassee, Florida. Established "way back" in 1992, this community network was designed from the beginning to encourage large, local information providers to establish their own information servers that would link together through the Free-Net system.

Three Rivers Free-Net (trfn.clpgh.org) in Pittsburgh, Pennsylvania, is sponsored by the Carnegie Library of Pittsburgh. TRFN represents a large, well-supported library system reaching out to draw in partners in order to provide twenty-first-century services to its local community.

Trails (trails.net/) is another rural, consortial project in Southeast Kansas. The unique twist there is the implementation of a wireless network to link the public library, city hall, two additional city buildings, and chamber offices to a direct leased line provided by a local telephone company for a shared Web server and community wide area network.

You will find aspects of these (and many other) community networks highlighted throughout this book. Hyperlinks to these and other pertinent sites are available from my Web site (www.libsci.sc.edu/stephen/bajjaly.htm). As your time, interest, and needs permit, I strongly encourage you to "visit" these communities online. As the familiar slogan goes, "let your fingers do the walking." Then incorporate what you find into your own community networking efforts.

Community Assessment

Before undertaking the business planning process, the steering committee should complete a community assessment in order to ensure that the ensuing business plan for the community network is based upon solid data. The idea behind community assessment is that every community has at least some assets it can use to start building its own future. Community assessment determines what already exists in terms of knowledge and resources as the basis for what services to develop. It is the job of the steering committee to gather information from and about the community before determining what community networking services should be offered.

Ultimately, the ability of the community network to provide these needed services will depend upon the collaborative partnership arrangements that can be forged. According to Donald Littrell of the Missouri Express project, "A very practical reason for community assessment is that it can start the process of community ownership. People are much more likely to invest in the process when they realize that they do have resources that can make a difference and understand that they are valued partners in a process of development."[5]

Maurie Kelly, Assistant Documents Librarian at the University of Illinois–Chicago, suggests there are numerous sources of information available to profile a local community including population, housing, social, and economic statistics; business information; crime statistics; education and school data; health-related information; and maps.[6] She details many useful resources to consult in completing a community profile including:

1. U.S. Government sources
   a. U.S. Bureau of the Census, Census of Population and Housing: data on population, age, race, gender, employment,

education, income. The census tract option should be used when creating a community profile.

b. U.S. Bureau of the Census, Economic Censuses: Zip-code order information on manufacturing, retail trade, and services.

c. U.S. Federal Reserve board. Federal Financial Institutions Examination Council. *HMDA: Aggregate Report:* data on loans made by financial institutions, organized by metropolitan statistical area.

2. State and local government agency publications
   a. Board of Education (state and local)
   b. Employment security/Job service
   c. Housing
   d. Human services
   e. Management and budget
   f. Planning and development
   g. Police
   h. Public health
   i. Public schools
   j. Recreation

3. Community organizations

4. Cartographic resources
   a. Fire insurance maps
   b. U.S. Census Bureau Tiger/line data can be used to create maps using census data
   c. U.S. Geological Survey
   d. U.S. Library of Congress, Geography and Maps Division, *Fire Insurance Maps in the Library of Congress Checklist*

5. Commercial publications
   a. *Index to Current Urban Documents, A Guide to Local Government Publications.* Westport, Conn.: Greenwood Publishing Group.
   b. *Market Profile Analysis: Consumer and Business Demographic Reports.* Naperville, Ill.: First Data Solutions.
   c. Newspapers

Developing a Business Plan

Like any business hoping for long-term sustainability, you need to develop your community network with an eye to the future. The most comprehensive method for accomplishing this future forecasting is to develop a business plan based upon the results of a community needs and capabilities assessment. The goal of the steering committee is to create the Community Network Business Plan. The business plan tells people what you plan to do and how you plan to do it. Creating a business plan indicates to others that you are serious in your intentions and have thought about how to go about it.

The business plan can serve many functions:

To let the community know about the proposed community network and the services it will offer

To help the steering committee establish the community network and (later) the operating board to run the community network

To show potential partners and funding organizations why their support is necessary, where their support will be used, and what outcomes their support will deliver

To show community networking staff and volunteers what they will be doing

Developing a business plan often takes a long time but is not a particularly difficult task. It involves collecting a fair amount of information and then organizing that information into a workable, usable plan. The steering committee should plan a series of meetings in order to complete the various components of the business plan.

Since the community network is essentially an information system for the community, you can apply the same concepts of information systems planning that an organization would use to develop its internal information systems. You just broaden these concepts to think of the community as a whole instead of your individual organization.

Information systems planning is intended to achieve several objectives:

To set a strategic direction for the use of computers and telecommunications focused on your community in particular

To establish a vision for the future use of technology in the community

To achieve the support and commitment of the community's leaders and chief decision makers

To establish the criteria upon which decisions will be based

To ensure quality

To allocate funds and equipment appropriately

Information systems planning is important for many reasons:

It is the only way to manage change effectively.

It allows better management of information systems resources.

It improves communication between planners and users.

It brings control to a potentially complex and chaotic situation.

It influences the future.

On the other hand, if you do not plan, you take on many risks:

Improper hardware or software choices

Incompatibility problems within or between information providers and users

Ineffective or inefficient technical support

Duplication of effort—waste of resources

Limited impact of technology

Information systems planning should follow a "top-down" development approach. That is, you want to consider the big issues first. Start by conceptualizing in general terms. Only later on will you get into specific details. This top-down approach gives you two important benefits: (1) it will help to ensure that whatever technology solutions you devise will address real problems in your community and (2) it will more than likely force you to understand the situation first before considering the available options.

As you begin, there are three important questions to keep in mind and to be sure you can answer:

What are the information needs of the community and its citizens?

What is the technology available to meet those needs?

What can a community network do to match these two?

Therefore, your initial plan should pull together information on community objectives, user needs, and technological trends and determine the role of the community network in addressing the community's objectives and users' needs. It should also:

Be concise—no one has the time or interest to read through an unreasonably long plan

Include only useful information—if you focus on what is absolutely necessary, the plan will be only as long as necessary

Be self-contained—do not force your readers to hunt down additional documentation

You should strive to have your plan achieve the following objectives:

- Articulate the vision
- Inventory the present state of technology *use*
- Develop a guiding framework for the future
- Prepare implementation plans
- Measure and evaluate progress

Some thoughts to keep in mind as you work to develop the plan:

Link technology to general goals; remember technology is just a means to an end.

Focus on the future—not the past.

Be politically aware. Ensure buy-in at each stage of the plan's development from all important stakeholders. Communicate what you are up to; document your efforts.

Keep the time horizon relatively short.

Avoid too much detail.

Emphasize goals and objectives, not hardware and software purchases.

Avoid jargon and "techno-speak."

Be honest with yourself. Try to achieve what is reasonable.

According to guidelines issued by the Corporation for Public Broadcasting, a standard community network business plan should include six elements:

1. Community network mission
    a. What is the purpose of the community network?
    b. How does this mission complement or supplement the missions of its founding sponsors?
    c. What are the potential strengths and weaknesses of the community network?
    d. Who or what is the competition? How does the community network project compare to this competition?
    e. How will the community network complement or supplement similar programs on the local, regional, state, or national level?

2. Environment and marketplace
    a. What competition exists for the community network?
    b. How will the community network differ from its competition?
    c. How will the community network complement or compete?
    d. What are the existing marketplace opportunities? the threats?
    e. What action will the board (or network administrators) take in response to these opportunities or threats?
    f. What are the critical success factors for long-term sustainability?
    g. What strategies are available to the community network to ensure success?
    h. What tactics will the board (or network administrators) use to apply these strategies? How will these tactics and strategies be altered, if necessary?

3. Administrative team
    a. What are the staffing requirements?
    b. How do these staffing requirements meet the service needs (e.g., administrative, technical, training, volunteer management, marketing/PR, etc.) of the community network?
    c. How will these service needs and their associated staffing requirements change over the next three to five years?
    d. How will the network obtain sufficient human resources to achieve its objectives? Full-time employees? Part-time employees? Volunteers? Consultants? Professional service agreements?

   e. What organizations, services, networks, educational institutions, or other entities will participate in the network? What are their roles in the project? How will their roles change over the next three to five years?

4. Marketing plan
   a. Who are the potential consumers/users of the community networking initiative?
   b. Who does or will have access to this initiative?
   c. What demographic segments of the consumer/user community (e.g., age group, lifestyle, interests, or other category) are being targeted? What racial and/or ethnic minorities are included?
   d. How will the board measure the needs or wants of the consumers/users? (Once the network is operational, the board might ask these questions: How satisfied are the consumers/users? Are the consumers/users recommending the network to others? How effective is the marketing plan for the community network?)

5. Financial plan
   a. Develop a project budget for the next three to five years that projects major-category revenues and expenses. (More details about budgeting are addressed in chapter 6.)
   b. Include best-case, expected, and worst-case scenarios over the three-to-five-year time span. Explain how the worst-case scenario will be addressed.
   c. Provide rationales for budget line item increases or decreases that exceed 10 percent yearly.
   d. What steps will the board take to maximize revenues and minimize expenses?
   e. What effect will these budget projections have on the administrative, financial, and operational needs of the network?
   f. What effect will these changes have on staff salaries and benefits?
   g. What will the marketing plan cost to implement?
   h. When will current equipment need to be replaced?
   i. What new equipment will be needed?
   j. What funding sources are available and how much will they invest?

    k. What could prevent the network from realizing its projected revenues?

6. Evaluation

    a. What objectives and milestones will the board use to measure progress in community network services use, financing, and marketing?

    b. What measures will alert the board (and others) that the community network is not operating according to schedule or that the project needs additional attention?[7]

The complete business plan should also include:

Executive Summary—a brief description of the overall business plan.

Community Needs Assessment—Why the community needs the community network. This should include an assessment of the community's level of understanding about technology and online communications; a determination of the community's interest in supporting community networking initiatives; and an inventory of the current level of publicly available technology. Includes a description of the techniques used to gather information.

Operational Details—The governance structure, operating staff requirements, start-up and ongoing operational requirements, technology infrastructure, project time lines, anticipated problems, and proposed solutions.

For More Information

The Board Member's Guide to Strategic Planning: A Practical Approach to Strengthening Nonprofit Organizations, by Fisher Howe. San Francisco: Jossey-Bass, 1997. ISBN: 0787908258.

Building Credibility with the Powers That Be: A Practical Guide to Enhanced Personal, Program and Organizational Power, by Gail Moore and Marilyn MacKenzie. Downers Grove, Ill.: VMSystems-Heritage Arts Publishing, 1990.

Changing by Design: A Practical Approach to Leading Innovation in Nonprofit Organizations, by Douglas C. Eadie. San Francisco: Jossey-Bass, 1997. ISBN: 078790824X.

Community Network Planning Guide. (www.bev.net/project/evupstart/planning.html)

Measuring Community Capacity Building: A Workbook-in-Progress for Rural Communities. (www.aspeninst.org/dir/polpro/REPP/ REPPPubs.html#1)

Missouri Express Resource Guides. (outreach.missouri.edu/moexpress/guides/)

Guide 2: What Are Community Networks? by Ted L. Gallion

Guide 3: Frequently Asked Questions, by Ted MacDonald

Guide 4: Getting Started, by Mary Simon Leuci

Guide 5: Establishing a Direction: Shared Principles, Purpose, Vision, by Mary Simon Leuci

Guide 6: Developing an Action Plan Based on Purpose and Vision

Guide 7: An Introduction to Community Assessment, by Donald Littrell

Guide 8: Community Technology Profile, by Joe Lear and Ted MacDonald

Guide 9: Developing an Organizational Capacity Profile, by Mary Simon Leuci

Neighborhood Networks Resource Planning Guide. (www.hud.gov/nnw/nnwhowto.pdf)

The Organization of the Future, edited by Frances Hesselbein, Marshall Goldsmith, and Richard Beckhard. San Francisco: Jossey-Bass, 1997. ISBN: 0787903035.

An Organizational Strategy for Electronic Democracy, by Steve Miller. (www.ctcnet.org/stevemil.html)

Paradoxes of Group Life: Understanding Conflict, Paralysis, and Movement in Group Dynamics, by Kenwyn K. Smith. San Francisco: Jossey-Bass, 1987. ISBN: 155542046X.

Reinventing Citizenship: The Practice of Public Work. (www.cpn.org/CDC/reinventing_cit.html)

This report draws upon the experience of participants in a pilot project to illustrate the potential of active citizenship for reinvigorating public institutions and public problem solving. These are supplemented by books, articles, and other resources listed in its appendixes. Prepared by the staff and partners of the Center for Democracy and Citizenship, Humphrey Institute of Public Affairs, University of Minnesota, Twin Cities Campus, 301 19th Avenue South, Minneapolis, MN 55455; Phone: 612/625-0142; Fax: 612/625-3513.

The Skilled Facilitator: Practical Wisdom for Developing Effective Groups, by Roger M. Schwarz. San Francisco: Jossey-Bass, 1994. ISBN: 1555426387.

Strategic Management in Nonprofit Organizations, by Robert D. Hay. New York: Quorum Books, 1990. ISBN: 0899305512.

Strategic Management for Nonprofit Organizations: Theory and Cases, by Sharon M. Oster. New York: Oxford University Press, 1995. ISBN: 0195085035.

Strategic Management of Public and Third Sector Organizations: A Handbook for Leaders, by Paul C. Nutt and Robert W. Backoff. San Francisco: Jossey-Bass, 1992. ISBN: 1555423868.

Strategic Planning for Not-for-Profit Organizations, by R. Henry Migliore et al. New York: Haworth Press, 1995. ISBN: 1560249196.

Strategic Planning for Public and Nonprofit Organizations: A Guide to Strengthening and Sustaining Organizational Achievement, Revised edition, by John M. Bryson. San Francisco: Jossey-Bass, 1995. ISBN: 0787901415.

NOTES

1. Material in this section is adapted from *Missouri Express Resource Guide 5, Establishing a Direction: Shared Principles, Purpose, Vision,* by Mary Simon Leuci. (outreach.missouri.edu/moexpress/guides/)
2. *Turf Wars: Moving from Competition to Collaboration,* by Harvey Robbins. Glenview, Ill.: Scott, Foresman, 1990. ISBN: 0673460797.
3. Material adapted from "The Seamless Web and Democracy: Pre-Virtual Decisions and the Development of a Community Network," an unpublished paper by Mary Virnoche, University of Colorado at Boulder. Used with permission.

4. *Assessment and Evolution of Community Networking,* by Mario Morino. Copyright 1994 by Morino Institute. Used with permission. (www. morino.org/publications/assessment.html)
5. *Missouri Express Resource Guide 7: An Introduction to Community Assessment,* by Donald Littrell. 1997. (outreach.missouri.edu/moexpress/ guides/moexp7-1.html)
6. "Profiling a City: Information Resources on Chicago's 77 Community Areas," by Maurie C. Kelly. *Journal of Government Information* 23, no. 1 (Jan/Feb 1996): 1–11.
7. Adapted from *Business Plan Guidelines,* Attachment G: CWEIS Grant Contract, Corporation for Public Broadcasting, 1994.

4

Developing Community Partnerships

The cornerstone of any community network is that it is a collaborative, community-based activity. No one organization in the community should try to "go it alone" to establish or maintain the community network. Three primary reasons underscore this need for collaboration and help to ensure the community network's overall success:

No single organization encompasses the range of skills necessary to develop the community network.

If just one organization is involved, the community will perceive the community network as just an extension of the sponsoring organization's activities and will support it and participate accordingly.

Basing the community network within a single sponsoring organization subjects the community network to the future funding priorities of the sponsor and the service activities of the sponsor's governing board.

Community networking initiatives must coordinate a variety of tasks in order to be successful. By developing a successful partnership, the community network can draw on the distinctive competencies of each of its partners. That is, each partner organization contributes what it is best able to do or provide. For some, it may be technical expertise. For others, it may be fundraising. For another it may be working with a particular constituent group (e.g., children, seniors, the disabled).

In the case of MidNet (and I think for many other community networks), the critical element we relied upon the library to provide was public access. This was essential in enabling local residents to learn about MidNet, try it out, learn how to use it, contribute information, et cetera. Of the three sponsoring organizations, the library was the only partner used to or readily equipped for dealing with the public at large. Even though South Carolina ETV has a huge audience overall, it connects with this audience through its radio and television stations—not in direct face-to-face contact. Similarly, the University of South Carolina deals directly with its students, faculty, staff, and alumni—not directly with the general public.

Collaboration

To be sure, collaboration is not easy. But the basic tenets of community networking demand the support, cooperation, and participation of numerous community organizations. Your initial goal is to get a collaborative effort started in your community or to become an integral part of whatever community networking initiative is already underway. Your ongoing goal is to ensure that a synergy is developed and maintained between what the library seeks to do for the community and the community network's goals and objectives. The broad goals for any community network are to improve the quality of life for all citizens of the community and to enhance the local economy. How these broad goals are accomplished is up to you—and your collaborative partners.

Alvin Zander has been researching and writing about group behavior for the past fifty years. In his popular book, *Making Groups Effective,* Zander applies the results of ongoing psychological research to the practical problems that groups face every day. While the book does not offer any strict methodologies, it does describe how you can create conditions favorable for accomplishing group activities and avoid negative situations. Since effective partnerships are a critical success factor for community networking, I highly recommend the entire book.

According to Zander, "a group is a set of persons who interact with and depend on each other—who collaborate and behave in ways that suit mutual expectations."[1] A group will be weak if its members are more concerned with their own individual accomplishments than with the group as a whole; if they perceive the other members as rivals; if they are unconcerned with other members' activities; and if they are often absent from group activities. As the convener of a community networking steering committee, it is your objective from the start to bring together and organize the members into a strong, cohesive group.

Four conditions are typically necessary before a group is likely to form:

Some condition or situation exists that needs to be changed or corrected. For instance, as we head into the twenty-first century, the importance of online information and communication services continues to grow. As a professional concerned with equitable access to information, you want to ensure that all the residents of your community can participate.

Perception of a solution to the condition or situation and steps to achieve it exist. For instance, a community network presents a viable strategy for you to meet the online information and communications needs of your community.

Members perceive the way to improve the situation is through group activities. By definition, a community network is a collaborative effort among the organizations and citizens of a community.

Environmental conditions support the establishment of the group and participation in its activities. For instance, the community network's sponsors are willing and able to follow through on their commitment of resources. The members of the steering committee willingly participate and are given the support necessary to participate effectively.

According to Zander, a strong group—that is, one that is well equipped to meet its objectives—exhibits four main attributes. A strong group (1) has the necessary social power to achieve its objectives and has members who (2) interact freely, (3) depend upon one another, and (4) want to remain a part of the group.

Strategies for Successful Partnerships

The following strategies are useful tools to use in order to create successful partnerships:

  Keep the group no larger than twenty, preferably seven or eight. Keeping the group small means more members are likely to talk to one another.

  Increase interactions between group members by leaving time on the agenda for discussion. Call for it and welcome it. Give members a chance to gather ideas in subgroups.

  Involve from the outset both people who are good at broad policy development and people whose strength is in detailed implementation activities.

  To keep the commitment of your partner organizations' leaders, involve them in determining how the community network is benefiting the community and how to institutionalize these benefits.

Organizations that decide to "partner" to develop a community network can establish one of three arrangements: cooperation, coordination, or collaboration. These relationships vary in their level of formality—cooperative relationships are at the informal end of the continuum; collaborative relationships at the other. Distinctions are made between the levels of shared authority, resources, risk, and rewards.

  Cooperation—This relationship is informal; there is no commonly defined mission, structure, or planning effort. Information is shared between the cooperating organizations but each organization retains its own distinct operating authority. Since resources are separate, there is virtually no risk in cooperating, but the rewards are distinct, too.

  Coordination—This relationship is more formal; there is an understanding of compatible missions between the coordinating partners. This relationship requires the establishment of formal communication channels since some mutual planning and division of roles occurs. While authority still resides in the individual organizations, there is some risk: resources are available to all coordinating partners and the rewards are acknowledged mutually.

Collaboration—This relationship is the most durable and pervasive of the three. Collaborative relationships bring previously separate organizations into a new structure with full commitment to a shared mission. These relationships require comprehensive planning and well-defined communication channels operating on many levels between the collaborative partner organizations. The collaborative structure itself determines authority. Risk is much greater since each partner contributes some of its own resources and reputation to the collaboration. Resources for the collaboration are pooled or jointly secured. The rewards are shared, too.

The success of most community networks—both in the beginning and in the long run—rests on its ability to find partners willing to work together to get the network up and running and to sustain it. Sustainability means that the network is established as a viable community resource—built from partnerships that supply the necessary expertise and guarantee operational funding well into the future.

A collaborative relationship is one that exhibits the following characteristics:

- Commitment to mutual relationships and common goals
- Jointly developed structure and shared responsibility
- Mutual authority and accountability for success
- Sharing of resources and rewards

Paul Mattessich and Barbara Monsey, upon reviewing a number of research studies, identified nineteen distinct factors that the studies found to influence positively the success of collaborations in human service, government, and other nonprofit organizations. In addition to describing each factor and its implications for potential collaborators, Mattessich and Monsey indicate the relative importance of each factor by noting the number of times it was mentioned across the various research studies they examined. The most important factors are identified by italics in the list below.* I strongly recommend you obtain and read the entire book since it includes important details not covered here.

---

* From *Collaboration: What Makes It Work,* by Paul Mattessich and Barbara Monsey, copyright 1992 Amherst H. Wilder Foundation. Used with permission. For more information on Wilder Foundation publications, call 1-800-274-6024.

Environmental Characteristics: describes the physical and social context within which the collaboration takes place. While group members may exert some influence over these factors, they are largely outside the group's control.

1. *History of collaboration or cooperation in the community*
2. Collaborative group seen as a leader in the community
3. Political/social climate favorable

These factors were verified by my interviewees. Many interviewees mentioned that they had collaborated previously with their current partners and/or spoke of the need to sell the collaboration to key community leaders in order to create the best possible climate for success.

Membership Characteristics: describes the individuals who compose the collaborative group as well as the organizations that form the collaboration.

4. *Mutual respect, understanding, trust*
5. *An appropriate cross-section of members*
6. Members see collaboration in their best interest
7. Ability to compromise

These factors were verified by my interviewees. Many of my interviewees indicated that their successes depend upon having collaborative members who sufficiently represent the community. Laying the proper foundation for a collaboration to succeed takes time. Collaborative partners need to enjoy being together and working to achieve the goals of the collaboration.

Process/Structure: refers to the collaborative's underlying management, decision-making, and operational systems.

8. *Members share a stake in both process and outcome*
9. *Multiple layers of decision making*
10. Flexibility
11. Development of clear roles and policy guidelines
12. Adaptability

My interviewees mentioned over and over that it was not enough to have their organizations' leaders get together to sustain the collaboration. It is important to have talented staff from within the organizations work on the collaboration and that these staff be invested in the collaboration and interested in its success.

Communication: how the collaborative members share information, keep each other informed, and express their opinions about the group's actions and activities.

13. *Open and frequent communication*
14. Established informal and formal communication links

My interviewees often noted the importance of getting stable representatives from each collaborating organization to ensure that strong links between members have a chance to form and to gel.

Purpose: why the collaborative group was formed, the results the collaboration seeks to achieve, and the tasks deemed necessary to achieve its goals.

15. *Concrete, attainable goals and objectives*
16. Shared vision
17. Unique purpose

My interviewees noted the importance of formulating clear goals upon which they could all agree. The mission and goals of the collaboration can overlap with those of its sponsoring organizations but must be distinctive in some way.

Resources: the financial and human capital necessary to develop and sustain a collaborative effort.

18. *Sufficient funds*
19. *A skilled convener*

Many interviewees noted the importance of financial stability and the important role of the leader of the collaborative effort when discussing what made their community networking efforts successful.

In summarizing their research, Mattessich and Monsey note that there is no simple answer to uncovering the right mix of factors. In general, the most important factors are the membership characteristics, but many factors are interrelated so changing one can have an effect on others. While these researchers caution that the influence of each factor should not be determined solely on the basis of how many times it was mentioned in the research studies, this does provide a rough measure of importance. "Research on collaboration is still in the early stages, and future studies may provide a better understanding of the true importance of each factor. The bottom line is: to ensure the effectiveness of your collaborative effort, pay attention to all the factors listed" (p. 11).

To learn more about how to establish and maintain successful community collaborations, I would recommend *Collaboration Handbook: Creating, Sustaining, and Enjoying the Journey,* written by Michael Winer and Karen Ray, also published by the Amherst H. Wilder Foundation. This handbook applies the factors identified by Mattessich and Monsey and walks you step by step through each activity necessary to achieve a successful collaboration.

Choosing Your Partners

The U.S. Department of Housing and Urban Development (HUD) suggests the following guidelines for choosing project partners:

> Draw partners from more than one source. Canvass your community and look for potential partners and volunteers from a variety of sources including schools and colleges, nonprofit organizations and charities, community organizations, churches, foundations, businesses, government agencies, and the media. Select partners from at least three of these categories.

> Partners must benefit too. Always be able to answer a potential partner's question, "What's in it for me?" Develop a plan to approach each potential partner with expected benefits, such as creating favorable publicity, better fulfillment of the partner's community mission, or development of a new consumer market or expansion of an existing base.

> Building partnerships requires a team approach. Everyone interested in developing the community network must be involved in identifying and soliciting partners. The steering committee should form a partnership development plan and help provide the labor needed to solicit each partner individually. Network

staff are essential for maintaining partnership contacts and identifying new sources for funding and support.

Partners are readily attracted to networks that already have stable sources of financial support. Multiyear commitments of money, volunteers, or in-kind contributions make a community network more sustainable and are likely to attract even more support if partners are confident their money is well invested. Strong alternative sources of funding, such as user fees, will also help convince partners that the network is a successful endeavor and well worth their support.[2]

Doug Schuler, author of *New Community Networks: Wired for Change,* offers good advice if you wish to become involved but live where a community networking initiative is already underway:

> For those actively interested in helping to develop community networks, it is a good idea to begin gathering information about the project. This can be done by attending the meetings, talking to the people, logging on to the system, and getting copies of brochures, policy statements, principles, and whatever else is available. . . . Give community network developers some benefit of the doubt as you are assessing their project. Developing a project democratically with limited resources and a largely volunteer base is far from easy. . . . Your input may be better informed and better received after you have spent some time with the project.[3]

Library Partnerships

This section profiles selected library/community network partnerships across the United States and Canada. I hope you will take the time to investigate these communities online and use them as springboards to developing a successful partnership for your own community. Keep in mind that these profiles represent only a very small portion of the accessible online communities—a number that grows with each passing day.

COIN, the Columbia Online Information Network (www.coin. missouri.edu) serving the residents of Columbia, Missouri, was established by the following sustaining members: the City of Columbia, Columbia Public Schools, Boone County, Daniel Boone Regional Library, and the University of Missouri–Columbia. The bulk of

COIN's budget is supplied by the sustaining members. These groups dedicate a portion of their annual budget to funding of COIN. The University makes an "in-kind" contribution: it houses the equipment, maintains it, and gives COIN a break on phone bills and service contracts that add up to the dollar value that the other organizations are contributing. Another large percentage of money is committed by affiliate members.

Columbia Free-Net (TCFN) (www.tcfn.org/) is a sustainable community network serving Southeastern Washington State. Franklin County provides dial-up phone lines, space, power, and networking expertise; BOSS Internet Group (a commercial ISP) provides free Internet service; and the Mid-Columbia Library (MCL) System provides a wide area network connecting eleven sites in three counties, with free local dial-up access. The MCL and the TCFN are interconnected so that citizens can travel freely from one system to the other. The Columbia Free-Net provides free e-mail to all residents, community information and resources, and free Web pages for noncommercial organizations.

KORRnet (www.korrnet.org), the Knoxville Oak Ridge Community Network serving the region around Knoxville, Tennessee, is very clearly a collaborative grassroots effort. Sponsoring organizations include the University of Tennessee, the Downtown Organization, Tennessee Valley Authority, Knox County, Knoxville and Oak Ridge city governments, the utilities board, the local newspaper, and a technology start-up. The executive director of the county library system serves on the KORRnet Board of Directors; the various public libraries host KORRnet's public access sites. A wide range of community agency representatives serve on the KORRnet operating committees.

LapeerNet (www.lapeer.lib.mi.us), based in rural Lapeer County, Michigan, began with the cooperative efforts of Lapeer County Intermediate School District and the Lapeer County Library to represent the county in a group now known as the Greater Thumb Telecommunications Consortium (GTTC). A request for support of a GTTC grant application spurred the county's Community Support Council to appoint a technology coalition. Representatives from government, nonprofit, and business concerns were charged to cooperatively address local technology infrastructure needs. The coalition has moved to make development and support of the community network and provision of training programs and public access sites its primary goals. The Mideastern Michigan Library Cooperative helped to secure funding for an Internet training center housed in the library administrative office as well as providing dial-in access and modems for K–12 schools, the public library, and the local community colleges. An experimental Web site was mounted and the first dial-in access in the county was established in 1994. The six school districts within the county pooled resources to purchase a server. They now share costs with the MMLC and the Lapeer County Library for the T1 connection and modem pool, with the library serving as the host facility.

ORION (www.orion.org/), the Ozarks Regional Information Online Network, was established in 1994 by the Springfield-Greene County Library, the City of Springfield, Regional Consortium for Education and Technology-Southwest, St. John's Health System, and Springfield Public Schools. To realize this vision, ORION is dedicated to providing a basic level of access, local public content, and training for users. To accomplish this mission, ORION provides a free access modem pool and public access terminals through the Springfield-Greene County libraries, with plans to develop other public access sites throughout the community. ORION's unique public content provides access to information about the Ozarks to Internet users worldwide. ORION's training programs help keep users abreast of the rapidly changing information technology. To continue its mission long term, ORION relies on organizational memberships (with various levels of enhanced telecommunication services), grants, and individual donations.

Three Rivers Free-Net (TRFN) (trfn.pgh.pa.us/). Citizens can access TRFN, based at the Carnegie Library of Pittsburgh, from any library in the county via the "Electronic Information Network" (EIN). EIN provides all residents of the county with equal access to the most up-to-date information for their education, employment, enjoyment, and health. This electronic network provides the county's libraries with cost-effective access to an electronic tool that enhances library planning, management, communication, and resource building and creates an electronically integrated library system. Collaborators on the EIN Project include the Carnegie Library of Pittsburgh, the Commission on the Future of Libraries in Allegheny County, and the Allegheny County Library Association.

Willard Public Library (www.willard.lib.mi.us/), Battle Creek, Michigan. Believing that the public library is the logical place for all citizens of any community to meet and care for its history, Willard Public Library has been actively promoting "community networking" in Battle Creek, Michigan, for many years. The foci of its efforts have been in the areas of developing collaborative relationships with other community organizations; becoming a center for community computer training and access; and collecting and disseminating information on the history of the area. The library believes strongly in the importance of developing collaborative relationships with other organizations in the community, both to enhance its mission and to provide better programming to its service area. It works with many groups toward mutually targeted goals, serving on various city and countywide initiatives and boards. The library provides office space and other services to two local networking organizations, the Calhoun County Non-Profit Alliance and the Great Lakes Free-Net. The library board has extended its support to these two organizations by adopting them as part of Willard Library under "assumed name" status. As a result of its efforts to mount advanced technology for the community, the Willard Public Library has become a de facto advisor to many other community organizations wishing to computerize their operations.

A story about another interesting community network, KooteNet (www.kootenet.net), was relayed to me by my friend and longtime community networking enthusiast, Steve Cisler. As I mentioned earlier, Steve is a librarian and a former Senior Scientist and Director of the Apple Library of Tomorrow (ALOT) program at Apple Computer Corporation. Steve continues to write and speak to groups all over the world about community networking.

> Lincoln County, Montana, is bounded by Canada to the north, Idaho to the west. The Kootenai River winds through the forests and mountains and two of the main towns, Troy and Libby. This is an isolated rural county, most of which is federal land. It is trying to become independent of the extractive industries that have come and gone, or at least downsized so much that a high school that once had 1,500 students now has about 800. Mills and mines have closed, but tourists still make their way to the campsites, lakes and lodges and wilderness areas. Transcontinental trains pass through the towns many times a day, but the drive to Helena, the capital, is more than six hours. Because of the brutal winters, especially recently, there are a lot of houses on the market. Outsiders fell in

love with the natural beauty, bought during the cool sunny summer season but vowed to leave after record snows.

I had been invited to give a talk at the Fourth Annual KooteNet Telecommunications Summit. What began as a small gathering of "geeks" had evolved into a real summit. About eighty adults from around the county attended the day long meeting.

KooteNet, a loosely formed nonprofit cooperative, is housed in a walled-off area of the library in Libby. The network administrator, Tony Pajas, is a retired veterinarian who returned to school to get a computer science degree in 1994, when the small team formed KooteNet. They sell dialup access to a T1 line (with a second one going in) for $14/month flat rate. They try to keep a user to modem ratio of about 10:1. With 1,200 households and 164 dialup lines they are doing even better.

KooteNet is doing well for several reasons. They pay a very high price for T1 service ($2,400 per month), yet they have dialup service (56kbps coming soon) at a price below the average. They have about 30 percent of the households signed up for accounts, and they have endeavored to measure the economic impact of the service and of new business generated by the connection. One amateur geologist and bookstore owner took his business to the Internet and sold over $100,000 worth of out-of-print books in 1997. Another artist closed his local gallery because he had so many Internet orders for his paintings and ship models that he could not keep up with the orders!

I was most impressed by the range of participants who came to the conference and then stayed to plan for the future. It seemed that all parts of the community were at the table as participants (except for the newspaper), including all the supervisors on the county board, and representatives from the lumber company, school, hospital, and a number of small businesses. Although she did not speak formally, Greta Chapman, the county library director, had a big part in organizing the meeting. She's one of those individuals in a small town that help determine its character, much more than a person with equal talents working in a larger city. I have met others all over rural America who at their best make me think about living in the places where they run their libraries.

After the conference Greta drove me and two staff members of the Montana state library to the Yaak River Valley, a very isolated area with a few hundred residents who now enjoy low-cost Internet service. It totally changes the nature of rural life. People feel they can maintain the independence prized so highly by Montanans, yet have the kinds of connectivity for information and communications enjoyed by people in urban areas. Yet the broadband services such as DSL and cable modems tend to be introduced in urban areas first. The independent telco in Libby talked about the XDSL services in Boise, but another speaker said that only 26,000 of the 200,000 phone lines in Montana would work with DSL equipment.

Even though the population seems to be a mix of progressives and conservatives, KooteNet has not had any big crisis about whether to use software filters or not. They are applying for E-rate funds, and of course there are bills in the hopper that could mandate some sort of filtering on computers used by children in libraries.

I don't want to make the mistake of trying to understand an area or its community network too quickly, but all of the impressions I had were good. Nobody had any criticism of the way the network functioned except a teacher who said that about 20 percent of the subscribers were Macintosh users, but the KooteNet employees provided no support for that platform. He added, "But that doesn't matter. The Mac users take care of each other." And isn't that the ideal? For people in a community to take care of each other? [4]

More information about various community networking partnerships is available on my Web site: www.libsci.sc.edu/stephen/bajjaly. htm. I started this project early into my community networking research in order to answer the question, "Who's community networking?" The goal has been to categorize the partnership arrangements of the established community networks across the United States and Canada. With the assistance of three (so far) of my graduate student assistants at the University of South Carolina College of Library and Information Science—Kari Maschoff, Joshua Crowe, and Jennifer Thompson—we have (1) examined several community networking-related Web sites to compile a comprehensive list of the existing community networks; (2) "visited" each site to determine what partners compose each network, how the network is funded, etc.; and (3) contacted each site's administrator to verify the correctness of our information-gathering efforts.

Our original goal was to determine how many community networks list the local library as a major partner. Over time, this investigation has grown to encompass a very large spreadsheet. Included at the end of each country is a subtotal of the number of community networks that fall within each of the partnership categories. Overall totals are contained at the bottom of the spreadsheet. This information is particularly instructive in giving you an overall "laundry list" of the types of organizations you should consider partnering with in your own community and the likelihood that approaching such organizations will come to fruition. A separate listing details the community network's full name, city, state or province, country, and any alternate name it goes by (if applicable).

Local Government Online

One of the most crucial partnership relationships, and yet often the most difficult to secure, is the relationship with local government. Most local governments are interested in anything that will save time and money—to enable them to lower (or, at least, not raise) taxes. The notion of "investing" in technology is still not widespread among local government officials. They also usually appear extremely averse to risk and are not overly interested in "innovation" per se. However, I would venture that local government oversees the single most important repository of information that truly affects people's lives on a daily basis. Therefore, it is never too early to do whatever you can to get them on board in support of your efforts.

As with other partners, you need to be able to articulate to local government the benefit it will receive from participating in the community network. In addition to cost cutting, government officials seem very interested in two items: quality of life and economic development, the two goals of community networking. I have found it helpful to review with local government administrators and political leaders what makes for a competitive region in the Information Age. That is, point out the benefits that can accrue from providing access to important information throughout the community (decentralization), providing everyone with access to the same information (equity), and working cooperatively to ensure that the information is consistent from one jurisdiction to another (collaboration). Similarly, you can impress upon them the benefits of "twenty-four-hour government"—that citizens will be able to access important information whenever the need arises. Show them other local governments that are online.

It can be hard to know who really are the decision makers and who really holds the power in local government. Even if you are clear on who needs to give the go-ahead, you may not get full support and cooperation the first time, but you need to persevere. You may find that local governments would rather deliver the information themselves and not as a part of the community network infrastructure. Try to point out the mutual benefits of cooperation. If that doesn't work, consider your efforts as contributing to the larger good: after all, having the information available somewhere is better than nowhere, isn't it?

The Austin Model

For inspiration, I once again turn to Austin, Texas—a place where the city of Austin is a key partner in community networking efforts. The City of Austin established the "Austin City Connection" (www.ci. austin.tx.us/) to deliver city information to citizens using the Web.

Key to the success of this endeavor is that the city manager and the Austin City Council set the pace for the development of this exciting new means of delivering services. Then a team of City of Austin employees (the Internet Task Force) worked with many of their fellow employees as well as various community partners to design and launch this service.

The ongoing success of the Austin City Connection is due in no small measure to the fact that regular city employees maintain and deliver pertinent online information for their departments. Employees "own" the Web site and, therefore, have a more vested interest in ensuring the quantity and quality of the information they deliver. Regular and sufficient training, support, and the necessary technical assistance are important factors to keep in mind. Off-loading information delivery to some third party—whether inside or outside the organization—is an inherently less successful model.

The Austin Internet Task Force adopted the following core principles to steer its work and the future development of the Austin City Connection. You may find these principles helpful when planning how to work with your own local government officials.

Core Principles

Focus on services, not technologies; on connecting people, not computers.

Ensure this new tool is easy and exciting for people to use.

Stimulate community participation and partnerships to ensure the opportunities and benefits of this new resource are available to everyone.

Remember that open, honest communication is key to participatory government and a livable community.

Guard the public trust by using resources responsibly and with respect for all people, property, and laws.

Do not try to do everything at once. Look to the City Council priorities and the community for direction, and remember that the people using this new resource will define it, enhance it, keep it vigorous, and make it meaningful.

Remember that the people of Austin make us a high technology leader.

Strategic Focus Areas

Content and interactive services—Build useful content and interactive services to demonstrate the possibilities.

Universal access—Partner with nonprofit and private sectors to catalyze and support universal access for citizens, reduce the gap between technology haves and have nots.

Staff access—Build internal network and systems capacity so employees in every department can use these tools to improve service.

The Indianapolis Model

Another online inspiration is the City of Indianapolis, Indiana. There, Mayor Stephen Goldsmith believes strongly in "e-government": providing online access to services and officials is the key to reinventing government for the twenty-first century. According to Goldsmith:

> You can't reinvent government—or pretend to—without the significant use of an Internet backbone. . . . Our site really has two uses: to reinvent government by more efficiently moving information inside City Hall . . . and second, to enhance the delivery of services to the citizens, so that eventually they wouldn't have to come [to City Hall].[5]

Mayor Goldsmith has set the pace for the Indianapolis/Marion County Web site (www.IndyGov.org/) by instructing the Web site development team to work with all city departments to deliver at least two new Internet services per week. In response, the team developed a five-phase system for defining the various types of information that the Web site will include. Each phase represents an increased level of interactivity, with each new service expected to be introduced at Phase Two or above:

Phase One—minimal interactivity; primarily general information such as agency contacts and phone numbers

Phase Two—increased accessibility; downloadable documents

Phase Three—improve a service by adding Internet tools such as e-mail access to government, develop interactive maps

Phase Four—fully Web-enabled service by making the business process interactive

Phase Five—streamline the delivery of a city service by reengineering the business processes for efficient delivery over the Web

Indianapolis's efforts were recognized by the 1997 Global Information Infrastructure award (www.gii.com/) in the "government" category.

✎ Good Ideas

Listed below are thoughts and suggestions passed along by my interviewees that relate to developing community partnerships:

- ✎ Become a detective and figure out who in the community is laying fiber optic cable. (Chances are it's the electric company.) Who is doing wireless communications? Using satellite dishes? Partner with them.

- ✎ Collaborating on developing the community network can change the image of the library from a "warm, fuzzy place" to that of technology leader in the community. Whenever later discussions about technology come up, the library will be an integral part of the discussion. Nothing can change the library more than involvement with community networking.

- ✎ Even if some groups don't want to get involved right away, keep them included because eventually they will want to get on board. Community networking can be the key to their long-run survival.

- ✎ Get involved with the key organizations and key players in the community long before starting any project (including the community network). Then look for ways to establish partnerships. Enable these other organizations to get to know the library as you—and not solely as the "building on the corner." As these organizations identify problems or needs in the community, you are there to help solve them. The implementation committee becomes library people along with chamber [of commerce] people, etc.

- ✎ If possible, take the lead in writing grants—this is a good way to stimulate the formulation of community partnerships.

➥ Incorporate the development of the community network as an outcome to a library-wide strategic planning process. Use this strategic planning process as a way to redefine how you plan to deliver library services in the future: examine every service, every service point. This will result in an established priority list that you can work from later.

➥ Involve government officials from the beginning. Meet with them face to face. E-mail is fine after a solid relationship has been established, but is not sufficient up front.

➥ It is easier to get the sponsoring organizations to continue to make the community network viable by reminding them that their customers want the services that the community network offers.

➥ It is very easy to approach the wrong people in any organization. Your initial tendency is to pitch to the data processing department. Yet the people who need to be involved are the people who do the PR—they understand getting the word out.

➥ It may take you a while to figure out where the library stops and the community network starts.

➥ Jump in with both feet—don't plan to death.

➥ Keep the community network's administrative structure fluid enough so that organizations are treated equally—regardless of when they come on board.

➥ Keep the start-up committee quite small—personalities really matter at this early stage of development. You need to be able to draw on the sheer energy of the personal relationships in order to get the collaboration going and sustained.

➥ Larger libraries seem to have more trouble establishing collaborative partnerships than do smaller, rural libraries. The problem for the small libraries is freeing up staff to perform community networking tasks.

➥ Libraries, schools, and colleges tend to be open organizations. Municipalities tend to be more compartmentalized, closed. It is far easier to sell the concept of community networking to open organizations.

➥ Specify the time commitments up front.

➤ Technology helps to break down the boundary issues between organizations.

➤ The collaborating organizations should all be equal when it comes to managing the community network.

➤ The importance of library involvement in community networking has less to do with Internet access than with politics. If the library is involved, it will be inextricably linked to the community network.

➤ The library is really already a community network. What other community computer networks can do is link to the library and vice versa. To do so, the library must be very proactive and forward-thinking.

➤ The library is the natural gathering place for community networking partners. The library has the "natural" ability to get others to participate.

➤ Try to get the participation of a local attorney, businessperson or chamber of commerce representative, and local government official. Even if they don't offer hands-on assistance, they can be valuable sources to "bounce" ideas off of. These people help you ensure you have the pulse of your community.

➤ View the community network as the way for your library to deliver the round-the-clock services that the public increasingly demands.

➤ You may not get all the groups to the table initially. Keep communications open so they won't feel excluded forever. On a regular basis, communicate with the nonparticipating organizations to let them know you're available, willing to do whatever it takes to move the process along.

➤ You must figure out how to talk to the people you need to talk to; how to establish trust. Then you can tell your partners what pieces you can do and what pieces you cannot do.

➤ You need to be out there so others feel comfortable to call. They see what your expertise is in a particular area. Become people's personal librarian and/or the librarian for the group. Always sell the library.

For More Information

This section is divided into two parts: general resources that relate to developing community partnerships and resources specific to local government.

General Information

Coalitions for Building Community Understanding.
  (www.cpn.org/sections/tools/manuals/NebGuide.html)

  This "NebGuide," published by Cooperative Extension, Institute of Agriculture and Natural Resources, University of Nebraska–Lincoln, is particularly focused on school-age child care. However, the process it discusses of involving the whole community is relevant to any area of policy-making. According to the authors, the process of building community understanding is an important one, regardless of the area of concern. As more and more citizens recognize a particular problem, that problem moves from the private to the public domain and requires the involvement of a larger segment of the community.

Collaboration: What Makes It Work, by Paul W. Mattessich and Barbara R. Monsey. Saint Paul, Minn.: Amherst H. Wilder Foundation, 1992. ISBN: 0940069024.

Collaboration Handbook: Creating, Sustaining, and Enjoying the Journey, by Michael Winer and Karen Ray. Saint Paul, Minn.: Amherst H. Wilder Foundation, 1994. ISBN: 0940069032.

Developing Community Resources on the Internet, funded by the Markle Foundation's Interactive Communications Technology Project. (www.markle.org/Markle+Foundation.nsf/vwHTML/Technology+Frame?OpenDocument)

  The goal of this project is to study the structure of local community resources on the World Wide Web and to develop models for future partnerships between nonprofit and commercial local Internet content providers. Products to date include:

  Community Resources: Self-Sustaining Online Models, by Peter Krasilovsky. 1998.

  Community Resources on the Web: Building Usage and Long-Term Viability, by Peter Krasilovsky. 1998.

Court Community Sites, Don't Ignore Them, by Steve Outing. 1998. (www.mediainfo.com/ephome/news/newshtm/stop/st070698. htm)

Local Community Partnerships with Community Sites, by Peter Krasilovsky. 1998.

Empowerment Zones and Enterprise Communities (EZ/EC). (www.ezec.gov)

This Web site details a Presidential initiative designed to afford communities real opportunities for growth and revitalization. Its mission is to create self-sustaining, long-term economic development in areas of pervasive poverty, unemployment, and general distress, and to demonstrate how distressed communities can achieve self-sufficiency through innovative and comprehensive strategic plans developed and implemented by alliances among private, public, and nonprofit entities.

The framework of the EZ/EC program is embodied in four key principles:

Economic Opportunity, including job creation within the community and throughout the region, entrepreneurial initiatives, small business expansion, and training for jobs that offer upward mobility;

Sustainable Community Development, to advance the creation of livable and vibrant communities through comprehensive approaches that coordinate economic, physical, environmental, community, and human development;

Community-Based Partnerships, involving participation of all segments of the community, including the political and governmental leadership, community groups, health and social service groups, environmental groups, religious organizations, the private and nonprofit sectors, centers of learning, other community institutions, and individual citizens; and

Strategic Vision for Change, which identifies what the community will become and a strategic map for revitalization.

Missouri Express Resource Guides. (outreach.missouri.edu/moexpress/guides/)

Guide 10: Building a Broad Base of Support and Involvement, by Mary Simon Leuci and Donald Littrell

Guide 11: Building Strategic Alliances and Partnering for Success, by
Mary Simon Leuci

Pew Partnership for Civic Change.
(www.cpn.org/sections/affiliates/pew_partnership.html)

This project is designed to help create innovative community collaborations between government, business, nonprofits, and citizens. To stimulate conversation about civic leadership, four
authors of diverse backgrounds are addressing the topic of building new civic leadership approaches within communities.

Building Healthy Communities.
(www.cpn.org/sections/tools/manuals/pew_healthy_com.
html)

Author Bruce Adams describes the elements of a healthy civic
community. Building on his background as an elected official,
Adams approaches his topic with examples of how citizen leadership works. By carefully delineating the contrasts between
productive and divisive communities, Adams lays a clear road
map for any community willing to invest in the effort of overcoming its internal turf wars.

Building Deliberate Communities.
(www.cpn.org/sections/tools/manuals/pew_delib_com.html)

Author Michael Briand introduces the reader to the role delib-
eration can play in creating new opportunities for communities to work together in more productive ways. Briand's
argument draws on statistical and educational research to
support the thesis that deliberative discussions can help a community learn its own strengths and weaknesses and can help
bolster its confidence in its ability to change itself for the better. Using a Community Convention as a vehicle, Briand's essay
explores the possibility of achieving a representative voice from
all community segments. Briand's brief description of his
experience with a Community Convention gives a firm example of what this vehicle can contribute.

Building Diverse Communities.   (www.cpn.org/sections/topics/
community/stories-studies/pew_diverse_com.html)

Author Jeanne Porter describes the importance of dialog in
developing community leadership among diverse groups. In
the context of South Carolina's Penn School for Preservation,

she highlights ways communities can create diverse leadership cadres working toward common goals and critiques common assumptions about the effectiveness of current leadership training methods.

Building Collaborative Communities.

Author Suzanne Morse concludes the series by exploring the importance of citizen involvement in creating sustainable collaborative partnerships within communities.

Local Government Information

The online resources listed below have been selected specifically to help you plan a strategy for increasing the amount of local government information available electronically.

The Alliance for Redesigning Government. (www.alliance.napawash.org)

This organization was founded in 1993 by a nonpartisan coalition of leaders to build an information network for people making government work. Based in Washington, D.C., the Alliance is part of the congressionally chartered National Academy of Public Administration, an established nonprofit dedicated to improving government at all levels.

Civic.com. (www.fcw-civic.com)

This Web site includes articles, "best practices," and other materials dealing with the use of information technology in state and local government.

"Government as a Model User," Chapter 8 in *Preparing Canada for a Digital World: Final Report of the Information Highway Advisory Council.* Published by Industry Canada, September 1997. (strategis.ic.gc.ca/SSG/ih01646e.html)

Government Technology Online. (www.govtech.net/)

This Web site provides publications, conferences, and other information about the uses of technology in government.

Innovations in American Government. (ksgwww.harvard.edu/~innovat/)

This Web site relates to an awards program of the Ford Foundation and Harvard University, administered by the John F. Kennedy

School of Government in partnership with the Council for Excellence in Government.

Institute for Electronic Government.   (www.ieg.ibm.com/)

This institute is designed to serve as a global resource for government leaders to explore, develop, and share strategies appropriate to our times—public policy, cyberlaw, economic development, electronic commerce, delivery of services to citizens, constituency relationships, and replacing industrial-age institutions with the art of governance—through digital age technologies and networks.

Local Government Institute (LGI).   (www.lgi.org)

LGI is a nonprofit organization dedicated to improving the quality of local government throughout the English-speaking world. To accomplish its mission, LGI provides technical assistance to local governments, develops "how-to" and reference manuals and software, and provides services, information, and advocacy to advance the quality, integrity, and professionalism of local government based upon sound principles of public administration. While LGI is concerned about all areas of local government, its principal focus is on human resources administration, governance, and community development. Of particular value is the "Links to Other Government Sites" page.

National Association of Counties.   (www.naco.org)

NACo was created in 1935 to give county officials a strong voice in the nation's capital. More than six decades later, NACo continues to ensure that the nation's 3,072 counties are heard and understood in the White House and the halls of Congress. NACo, the only national organization that represents county governments in the United States, continues to follow the traditions established by those early county officials. With its headquarters on Capitol Hill, NACo is a full-service organization that provides legislative, research, technical, and public affairs assistance to its members. The Web site includes a "Model Programs" database of projects in a variety of areas including economic development, information technology, and libraries.

National Performance Review.   (www.npr.gov)

This is the official name of the Clinton-Gore Administration's initiative to reform the way the federal government works. Its goal is to create a government that "works better and costs less." Begun in the early days of the administration, and with Vice President Al Gore at its helm, the Review has operated through several phases of initiatives.

Public Sector Continuous Improvement Site.
  (deming.eng.clemson.edu/pub/psci/)

This Web site aims to help public-sector employees improve their organizations by focusing on the variety of improvement methodologies. The site includes a guide to online resources for public-sector continuous improvement efforts; an online library of articles, reports, and case studies; information about organizations devoted to helping with public-sector improvement efforts; and links to related Web sites.

Smart Communities.   (www.smartcommunities.org)

This project, profiled in some detail in chapter 2, is a joint effort between the California State Department of Transportation (Caltrans) and the International Center for Communications at San Diego State University. This Web site includes a guidebook and implementation materials for communities interested in making better use of information technologies (i.e., the smart communities concept) as well as case studies of communities nationwide that have evolved into "smart communities."

State and Local Government on the Net.
  (www.piperinfo.com/state/states.html)

This Web site, produced by Piper Resources, offers a frequently updated directory of links to government sponsored and controlled resources on the Internet.

States Inventory Project.   (www.states.org)

This Web site has been designed to foster the development of the NII by providing a single clearinghouse for tracking state information infrastructure strategies and activities. By providing a resource for state-by-state comparative analysis, the States Inventory Project helps the states efficiently develop their own advanced telecommunications infrastructures. This resource is shared and maintained by state policy makers, telecommunications experts, and other interested parties.

NOTES

1. *Making Groups Effective,* 2nd ed., by Alvin Zander. San Francisco: Jossey-Bass, 1994.
2. Information in this section adapted from the HUD Neighborhood Networks document *How to Plan for Sustainability* (www.hud.gov/nnw/nnwtech4.pdf).
3. *New Community Networks: Wired for Change,* by Douglas Schuler. Reading, Mass.: Addison-Wesley, 1996, pp. 334–35. ISBN: 0201595532.
4. *KooteNet Telecommunications Summit Report,* by Steve Cisler. 1998. (home. inreach.com/cisler/libby.html). Used with permission. You can contact Steve or keep up-to-date on his travels and writings by accessing his home page (home.inreach.com/cisler/index.html).
5. *IndyGov.org Paves the Road to an Electronic City Hall,* by Christine Poulos. 1998. (govt-tech.govtech.net:80/gtmag/1998/may/bow/bow.shtm) See also Mayor Goldsmith's home page (www.ci.indianapolis.in.us/mayor_frameset.htm).

Managing a Community Network

Once the steering committee has developed the business plan, it is time to shift into "operational mode." Some members of the steering committee, including you, may decide that overseeing the ongoing operation of the community network is best left to others. Or the current members may decide to stay on. However it works, administering a community network presents new challenges altogether.

Community Network Administration

Many community networks have established a three-tiered administrative structure as shown below:

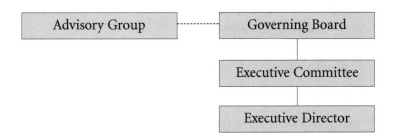

The advisory group is a largely ceremonial group of approximately twenty-five community leaders. They meet once or twice a year, mainly to demonstrate their support for the community network.

The governing board includes at least one representative from each of the community network's sponsoring organizations (e.g., library, local government, school) plus additional members if desired. This group, which meets quarterly, generally numbers from twelve to eighteen and is responsible for approving the overall implementation and service delivery plan.

The executive committee functions as the operating board of directors. As a subset of members from the governing board, this group, which generally meets every month, is charged with approving the administrative policies. This group generally includes the sponsors' representatives plus one or two additional members who rotate annually. The executive committee oversees the executive director, who is in charge of day-to-day operations of the community network. The executive director may have additional staff to supervise.

Peter Morgan, chairman of the board of the Chebucto Community Network in Halifax, Nova Scotia, and CEO of RiverSystems (www.riversystems.com), a training and development consulting firm, offers the following advice regarding the board's responsibilities and duties.

1. Members of your board should understand their responsibilities and duties prior to starting their term of office. These include:

    a. Understanding the mission, goals and objectives, and services of the community network
    b. Avoiding any conflict of interest or appearance of personal gain from serving on the board
    c. Attending regular board meetings whenever possible
    d. Becoming familiar with the financial infrastructure and operations (budget, budgeting process, fundraising activities)
    e. Determining who can disburse the community network's funds and in what amounts
    f. Ensuring that an annual financial audit is performed by a certified accounting professional

2. The board should ensure that any bylaws, policies, or procedures are written clearly and objectively and are implemented to include at least the following operating details:

    a. Personnel (including job descriptions and regular performance evaluations)

    b. Financial management (budgeting, revenue, expenses)

    c. Membership (dues, terms, eligibility requirements, privileges, etc.)

    d. Board or committee membership (duties, responsibilities, eligibility, term of office, etc.)

    e. Volunteers (duties, responsibilities, eligibility)

3. Since the board has a number of issues that must be addressed, it helps to articulate these formally in an action plan, complete with a timetable for implementation. Items to include in this action plan:

    a. Governance structure

    b. Staffing requirements

    c. User information services, training, and support

    d. Information provider recruitment, training, and support

    e. Public awareness

    f. Relationships with local, regional, and national computer networking, telecommunications, media, and other partners

    g. Evaluation plan[1]

Volunteer Management

Attracting, retaining, and making effective use of volunteers are very important activities for most community networks. Volunteers can be the most enthusiastic proponents and advocates for increased support and funding. Volunteers help spread the word to new groups of potential users and supporters about the benefits of getting online and participating in the community network. Volunteers make up that critical gap in people power between what is needed to meet the goals and what is affordable. Effective volunteer management is essential to ensuring a smooth operation.

Community networks use volunteers in many ways, including:

Clerical support—provide office assistance such as answering phones, assisting walk-ins, performing administrative support, running errands

Help desk—provide in-person, telephone, or online technical support and assistance to users and information providers

Information provider assistance—recruit, train, and assist individuals and organizations with information to contribute to the community network

Interactive services—moderate and manage online forums, chat sessions, discussion lists

Marketing and public relations—develop and implement activities to promote the community network

Public access—oversee and maintain public access terminals throughout the community

Recruitment—attract new users and supporters of the community network

Speakers' bureau—give presentations and demonstrations to groups and organizations

Technical support—maintain the community network's underlying computer and telecommunications systems

Training—develop and deliver one-on-one, small-group, and large-group orientation and training sessions

Keep in mind that the community network will be competing with many other worthy organizations for its volunteers. And managing community network volunteers is no different from managing volunteers in other nonprofit settings. Your objective is to match the work that needs to be done with people willing to do the work. To do this properly and have it be a winning situation all around, you must start with the clear intention to reach out to your volunteers and to treat them properly.

Community network administrators make the following suggestions for managing volunteers effectively:

Start with a monthly volunteer orientation session. This gives prospective volunteers a chance to "check you out" without having to make a firm commitment.

Schedule regular opportunities for your volunteers to get together—for meetings, idea sharing, social gatherings.

Start with a volunteer skills and availability profile. Computer knowledge? Organizational and leadership skills? Promotion and sales? Writing and design? Relevant experience? Availability: mornings, afternoons, evenings, weekends?

Provide regular training opportunities. If volunteers can perform well, they tend to continue. If not, they will leave.

Let volunteers rotate from area to area. Don't assume they want to stick with one task for too long.

Keep volunteers to a schedule. Show them they have a commitment to keep. Surely the schedule must be flexible, but it lets people know how important they are and how much you count on them.

Special events often attract talented volunteers—people who might not consider volunteering for the community network's day-to-day operations. There is something about helping with an event that is attractive to volunteers.

Volunteer Management Information Online

The online resources listed below have been selected specifically to help you plan a strategy for attracting, training, and recruiting volunteers for the community network.

Beacon Project (www.beaconproject.org/) is a nonprofit organization committed to providing quality management support services to community and nonprofit leaders so they may better serve their clients. This Web site provides "e-corps," a place for people to volunteer online that includes a discussion forum (for nonprofit managers to post questions), an electronic cohort (offering advice, strategic thinking, or whatever information the participants deem relevant), and a knowledge bank (articles or papers useful to a nonprofit manager or community leader).

Chicagoland Volunteer Opportunities (www.npo.net/nponet/volunt.htm).

Do Something (www.dosomething.org) inspires young people to believe that change is possible. Trains, funds, and mobilizes young people to be leaders who measurably strengthen their communities.

Energize, Inc. (www.energizeinc.com/ener/ener.html) provides a Web site exclusively devoted to volunteer management.

Hearts and Minds (www.heartsandminds.org/), through its Web site and national publicity efforts, is reaching out to motivate people to get involved, showing how to make volunteering and donations more effective.

Independent Sector (www.indepsec.org/) brings together foundations, nonprofit groups, and corporate giving programs to support philanthropy, volunteerism, and citizen action.

Impact Online (www.impactonline.org), a nonprofit corporation headquartered in Palo Alto, California, is designed to facilitate and increase community involvement via the Internet. Impact Online seeks to collaborate with and complement existing organizations and build community resources to get more people involved. This Web site includes useful information about "virtual volunteering."

Leaders in Furthering Education (LIFE) (www.life-edu.org/index.html) seeks to reward and encourage volunteering and leadership in young people.

Neighborhoods Online (libertynet.org/community/phila/natl.html) was created in 1995 by the Institute for the Study of Civic Values (libertynet.org/~edcivic/iscvhome.html) and Philadelphia's LibertyNet (libertynet.org) as an online resource center for people working to build strong communities throughout the United States. The aim of Neighborhoods Online is to provide fast access to information and ideas covering all aspects of neighborhood revitalization, as well as to create a national network of activists working on problems that affect us where we live.

Patch the Apple (www.patchtheapple.org/) exists to promote volunteerism and to organize fundraising and other charitable events to benefit social and human services groups in New York City.

Three Rivers Free-Net Volunteer Opportunities Page (trfn.clpgh.org/About/volunteer.shtml) provides descriptions of the various ways volunteers can help support the mission of the community network.

Volunteer's Legal Handbook (www2.polarnet.com/~jdewitt/vlh/) provides an overview of legal issues intended to help you determine when to seek professional advice.

Volunteer Web (www.epicbc.com/volunteer/) provides a variety of information services related to connecting volunteers with suitable opportunities and discussing issues of interest to agencies making use of volunteers.

↠ Good Ideas

Listed below are thoughts and suggestions passed along by my interviewees that relate to managing your community network:

- ↠ Consider the community network as a test bed for the reorganization of your internal management, since the community network gets people talking and linked horizontally in ways that have never happened before.

- ↠ Develop a staff that cares and is very customer oriented. Empower the employees to say yes. Let them bend over backward to go the extra mile.

- ↠ Develop clear job descriptions for your volunteers. Be realistic about their time commitments up front. They need regular support to become effective and to remain so. Ask them what they want: motivation, encouragement, training?

- ↠ Divide the requisite administrative duties among several committees. Make these committees sufficiently large so that the workload can be switched around or handed off to others.

- ↠ Don't expect a quick fix. Community networking takes a long time and considerable effort to sustain.

- ↠ Don't promise more than you can deliver.

- ↠ Establish and maintain a good, enthusiastic board of directors.

- ↠ Half of community networking is technology and content; the other half is people.

- ↠ Have each committee report its progress at each board meeting but otherwise let the committees administer themselves.

- ↠ Hire people with a good attitude. You can train them to do the rest.

- ↠ It is important to get people together, so have volunteer meetings, social gatherings, etc. Those involved with keeping the community network going accomplish a lot of idea sharing when they get together.

➤ It is very exciting to see how library staff apply the community network to their own lives. Once staff see the practical application and how the community network can enhance their jobs, they come on board.

➤ It's easy to get caught in the "it's never enough" mindset. For obvious reasons, you need to resist this. View the glass as half full: Be positive. Your endurance will be critical to your success.

➤ Lots of people in the community want to help but are unsure how they can contribute to the community network. Place importance on defining these useful roles and getting volunteers to fill them.

➤ New issues will always arise when it comes to community networking. It helps to go into all this with a plan for how issues will be resolved by the partners.

For More Information

Boards That Make a Difference: A New Design for Leadership in Nonprofit and Public Organizations, 2nd ed., by John Carver. San Francisco: Jossey-Bass, 1997. ISBN: 0787908118.

Community Information Service Management Guidelines, by infoWorks Partnership, 1996. (www.infowks.com/bookord.html)

This book is described as a complete resource dedicated to the design, development and daily operation of community information services. Recommended by Missouri Express as an "excellent resource for detailed development of policy, procedures, and operations."

Enhancing the Volunteer Experience: New Insights on Strengthening Volunteer Participation, Learning, and Commitment, by Paul J. Ilsley. San Francisco: Jossey-Bass, 1990. ISBN: 1555422896.

Governing Boards: Their Nature and Nurture, by Cyril O. Houle. San Francisco: Jossey-Bass, 1989. ISBN: 1555421571.

Human Resources Management for Public and Nonprofit Organizations, by Joan Pynes. San Francisco: Jossey-Bass, 1997. ISBN: 0787908088.

Leadership and Management of Volunteer Programs: a Guide for Volunteer Administrators, by James C. Fisher. San Francisco: Jossey-Bass, 1993. ISBN: 1555425313.

Managing Beyond the Quick Fix: A Completely Integrated Program for Creating and Maintaining Organizational Success, by Ralph H. Kilmann. San Francisco: Jossey-Bass, 1989. ISBN: 1555421326.

Managing the Nonprofit Organization: Practices and Principles, by Peter F. Drucker. New York: HarperCollins, 1990. ISBN: 0060165073.

Missouri Express Resource Guides. (outreach.missouri.edu/moexpress/guides/)

> *Guide 21: Developing Guidelines and Policies,* by Mary Simon Leuci and Ted MacDonald

> *Guide 22: Operations,* by Ted L. Gallion

> *Guide 23: Developing a Viable Organizational Structure,* by Mary Simon Leuci

National Center for Nonprofit Boards (NCNB).   (www.ncnb.org)

NCNB is a nonprofit, membership organization designed to help nonprofit board members and paid executive staff create healthy, powerful organizations. NCNB provides a variety of education and training programs, consulting services, and publications to members and nonmembers alike.

Nonprofit Governance: The Executive's Guide, by Victor Futter (general editor) and George W. Overton (managing editor). New York: American Society of Corporate Secretaries; Chicago: American Bar Association, Business Law Section, 1997. ISBN: 1570734224.

The Nonprofit Handbook: Management, by Tracy Daniel Connors. New York: Wiley, 1997. ISBN: 0471179671.

This book offers proven advice, from experts in the field, on every facet of a nonprofit's daily operations: management and leadership, human resources, benefits, compensation, financial management, marketing and communications, law and regulations.

Nonprofit Organization Handbook, 2nd ed., by Tracy Daniel Connors. New York: McGraw-Hill, 1988.

This handbook provides a wealth of operational information that could be useful to any community network board or manager.

Profiles of Excellence: Achieving Success in the Nonprofit Sector,
    by E. Burt Knauft. San Francisco: Jossey-Bass, 1991.
    ISBN: 155542337X.

Selected Bibliography for Nonprofits, by Indiana University Center
    on Philanthropy.   (www.iupui.edu/it/philanth/bigbib.html)

This bibliography provides annotated citations of print resources in philanthropy and nonprofit management in the following topic areas: periodicals; philanthropy tradition, history, and practice; planning and organizational effectiveness; public relations/marketing; financial management; human resources; fundraising; and board governance. Includes a list of publishers' addresses and phone numbers.

*The (Help!) I-Don't-Have-Enough-Time Guide to Volunteer
    Management,* by Katherine Noyes Campbell and Susan J. Ellis.
    Philadelphia: Energize, Inc. Available through the Society for
    Nonprofit Organizations' Resource Center (danenet.wicip.
    org/snpo), 6314 Odana Road, Suite 1, Madison, WI 53719,
    1-800-424-7367.

The Volunteer Management Handbook, by Tracy Daniel Connors.
    New York: Wiley, 1995. ISBN: 0471106372.

NOTE

1. Peter Morgan, "Creating an Effective Board of Directors" (RiverSystems, www.riversystems.com, photocopy). Used with permission.

Funding Issues

The success of your community network will ultimately depend on its ability to secure sustainable funding. That is, the network must find enough sources of revenue to cover its costs. Both start-up and ongoing operational costs must be considered and will vary depending upon the range and scope of services provided by the community network. The availability and likelihood of sustainable funding is an important aspect to consider when deciding what services the community network should provide, since it is not realistic to consider offering services unless you know how they will be funded. Sustainable funding remains the most challenging aspect of community networking.

The Costs of Community Networking

As a major component of the business plan, the steering committee must prepare two budgets. The start-up budget estimates the expenses necessary to get the community network up and running. Some of these expenses will occur one time or, at least, infrequently; others will recur on a regular basis. The operating budget details those recurring costs necessary to keep the network operational.

Start-up costs can vary greatly depending upon the services to be offered by the community network. Below is a basic checklist for items needed to establish a headquarters office for a community network.[1] Creating and maintaining budgets using a spreadsheet program such as Microsoft Excel will simplify the mechanical aspects of budgeting and give you an important advantage. Spreadsheets easily enable you to perform "What if?" analyses to test various expense/revenue scenarios.

Start-up Budget

1. Space needs
   a. Rent
   b. HVAC
   c. Partition walls
   d. Installation of closets, rest rooms, secure space

2. Furniture and equipment
   a. Desk and chair
   b. Computer table
   c. Work table
   d. Telephone
   e. Fax machine
   f. Photocopier
   g. Chairs
   h. Couch
   i. Lighting
   j. Bulletin board
   k. Coat rack
   l. Filing cabinets
   m. Antistatic floor coverings
   n. Carpet
   o. Signage

3. Computer hardware and software
   a. Server computer (including monitor, keyboard, and mouse)
   b. Administrative computer
   c. Printer(s)
   d. Computer projector
   e. Modem(s)

    f. Extended warranties and service contracts

    g. Software programs: word processing, spreadsheet, presentation, database, Web server, antivirus

4. Security

    a. Deadbolt locks on doors

    b. Locks: window, equipment, filing cabinets, closets

    c. Alarm system: installation and monitoring

5. Electrical considerations

    a. Expansion of power capacity

    b. Installation of electrical outlets

    c. Installation of overhead lights

    d. Installation of telephones and telephone lines

    e. Internet connection

    f. Computer cables, wires

    g. Extension cords

    h. Surge protectors

6. Insurance policies (general liability, property, Workmen's Compensation)

7. Office supplies

    a. Printing paper (letter and legal, white and colored)

    b. Photocopying paper (letter and legal, white and colored)

    c. Pads of paper

    d. Pens and pencils, crayons, colored markers

    e. Printer toner

    f. Soap, paper towels, toilet paper

    g. First aid kit

Many of the initial expenses will occur one time only. Others will continue to recur throughout the operation of the community network and require a yearly operating budget.

Operating Budget

1. Personnel

    a. Director

    b. Technical support

    c. Clerical

    d. Consultant fees

    e. Fringe benefits (determined by the organization)

2. Rent

3. Utilities

4. Insurance

5. Legal

6. Telecommunications

7. Travel

8. Equipment

9. Office supplies

10. Miscellaneous

Funding Options

The steering committee or operating board must also determine where the funding will come from to meet the expenses. Funding can come from the network's users or from potential sponsors and can be in the form of cash or in-kind contributions. The network uses the cash it receives to pay its outstanding bills. In-kind contributions are noncash donations of items or services needed by the community network that keep it from having to spend its available cash. Typical in-kind contributions include computer hardware and software, office space, legal and accounting services, marketing and public relations, etc.

According to Ted Gallion, author of Missouri Express Resource Guide 27, *Funding Options,* "When seeking resources, don't ask for 'contributions,' rather seek sources that will 'invest' in their own community. And when these resources are received, be prepared to report on their 'return on investment'—the outcomes."

Seek and ask for specific resources. Do not take a general approach when looking to fill a need. For instance, ask for two chairs for the public workstations at the senior center. Neil Yerkey, a founder of the Buffalo Free-Net, says "We have gotten several grants from our state legislators and a sizable grant from a communication company. These have come because people have seen the value of the system to the community, rather than from much success in writing formal grant proposals. Much of our continuing funding comes from small donations from users."

Community network funding comes from two primary sources: individuals and groups who benefit directly from the community network (i.e., its users) and those who want to improve the community and see the community network as a positive strategy to do this. These indirect beneficiaries include state and local governments, foundations, and corporations. According to Steve Cisler, "many community networks are currently witnessing a shift from reliance on grants to the resale of services. This is unfamiliar territory for many government and nonprofit endeavors."

Grant Writing

The Corporation for Public Broadcasting (www.cpb.org) evaluates hundreds of proposals each year for a variety of funding purposes. The information below is adapted from its Web publication, *Basic Elements of Grant Writing* (www.cpb.org/grants/grants.writing.html).

Successful grant writing involves the coordination of several activities, including planning, searching for data and resources, writing and packaging a proposal, submitting a proposal to a potential funding organization, and follow-up. Listed below are some steps that will help you to assemble high-quality proposals that have a greater likelihood of being funded. With more competition for funds than ever before, you need to do everything you can to ensure your proposals are given full consideration.

Preparation

You are likely to find preliminary grant writing steps to be the most time consuming, yet most vital, aspect of the process. If done well, your preparatory work will simplify the writing stage.

DEFINE YOUR PROJECT

Clarify the purpose of your project and write a mission statement. Define the scope of work to focus your funding search. Determine the broad project goals, then identify the specific objectives that define how you will focus the work to accomplish those goals. Decide who will benefit. Benefits may extend beyond the direct beneficiary to include the community, other institutions, etc. Draft expected project outcomes in measurable terms.

DEVELOP AN ACTION PLAN

The action plan combines the activities necessary to see the project through to completion with a time line for completing each of the activities. Be sure to include the planning phase, the period of searching for funds, proposal writing, and the intended project start date. Periodically update the action plan as you learn more about specific grant programs' submission deadlines, award timetables, etc.

DETERMINE YOUR PERSONNEL NEEDS

Based on the activities and timetable outlined in the action plan, identify required personnel both by function and, if possible, by name. Contact project consultants, trainers, and other auxiliary personnel to seek availability, acquire permission to include them in the project, and negotiate compensation.

IDENTIFY APPROPRIATE FUNDING SOURCES

Libraries, foundation centers, computerized databases, partner development officers, and publications are some of the resources available to assist your funding search. (Potential information sources are provided at the end of the chapter.)

Do not limit your funding search to one source. Look for a match between your project and the grants you seek by looking for consistency between the purpose and goals of your project and the potential funding organization. In addition, pinpoint specific funding priorities and preferences.

CONTACT POTENTIAL FUNDING ORGANIZATIONS

Make direct contact with funding organizations that support projects like yours.

Think of the funding organization as a resource. Identify a project officer who will address your questions. Request proposal guidelines as well as a list of projects previously funded. Perhaps an annual report is available. Inquire about the maximum amount available. Also, find out the average size and funding range of awards. Determine if funding levels of the grants you select are appropriate for your project. Note whether there is a funding floor or ceiling. Find out whether the funding organization has other grant sources for which your project is eligible.

Some funding organizations offer technical assistance, others do not. Ask for technical assistance, including a review of proposal drafts. Inquire about how proposals are reviewed and how decisions are made. Inquire about budgetary requirements and preferences. Are matching funds required? Is in-kind acceptable as a portion of applicants' share? What may be counted as in-kind, and how might it be applied? Learn about payment processes, including cash flow. Remember, the contacts you make may prove invaluable later, even if not now.

REVIEW THE PROPOSAL GUIDELINES

The proposal guidelines usually indicate submission deadlines, eligibility, proposal format (forms, margins, spacing, evaluation process and restrictions on the number of pages, etc.), review timetable, budgets, funding goals and priorities, award levels, evaluation process and criteria, whom to contact, other submission requirements. Read the guidelines carefully, then read them again. Ask the funding organization for clarification if necessary.

Plan to submit your proposal on or preferably before the deadline. Be realistic about whether you have time to prepare a competitive proposal that meets the deadline. Know the funding organization's policies on late submissions, exceptions, and mail delays. Find out how the funding organization will notify you about the receipt and status of your proposal.

UPDATE YOUR ACTION PLAN

Now that you know about submission deadlines and review timetables, factor ample time into your schedule. Consider how much time you will need to write multiple drafts, gather relevant and permissible materials, and prepare an impartial critique of your proposal for clarity, substance, and form.

Writing the Proposal

Structure, attention to specifications, concise persuasive writing, and a reasonable budget are the critical elements of the writing stage.

There are many ways to organize proposals. Read the guidelines provided by your potential funding source and follow the specifications about required information and how it should be arranged.

Standard proposal components are the narrative, budget, appendix of support materials, and authorized signature. Sometimes proposal applications require abstracts or summaries, an explanation of budget items, and certifications.

THE NARRATIVE

The narrative should include the following elements:

Statement of need—purpose, goals, measurable objectives, and a compelling, logical reason why the proposal should be supported. Background provides perspective and is often a welcome component.

Approach—method and process of accomplishing goals and objectives, description of intended scope of work with expected outcomes, outline of activities, description of personnel functions with names of key staff and consultants, if possible.

Method of evaluation—how and when results will be measured. Some funding organizations require very technical measurements of results. Inquire about expectations.

Project time line—paints a picture of project flow that includes start and end dates, schedule of activities, and projected outcomes. This portion of the narrative should be detailed enough to include staff selection and start dates.

Credentials—information about the applicant that certifies ability to successfully undertake the proposed effort. This typically includes institutional or individual track record and resumes.

Narratives typically must satisfy the following questions: What do we want? What concern will be addressed and why? Who will benefit and how? What specific objectives can be accomplished and how? How will results be measured? How does this funding request relate to the funding organization's purpose, objectives, and priorities? Who are we (organization, independent producer) and how do we qualify to meet this need?

Every narrative should contain a "hook." There are many ways to represent the same idea. However, the hook tailors the description of the idea to the interest of a particular funding organization. The hook aligns the project with the purpose and goals of the funding source. This is a critical aspect of any proposal narrative because it determines how compelling reviewers will perceive your proposal to be.

THE BUDGET

Budgets are cost projections. They are also a window into how projects will be implemented and managed. Well-planned budgets reflect carefully thought out projects. Personnel compensation is important budget information.

Funding organizations use these factors to assess budgets:

Can the job be accomplished with this budget?

Are costs reasonable for the market—or are they too high or too low?

Is the budget consistent with the proposed activities?

Is there sufficient budget detail and explanation? Many funding organizations provide mandatory budget forms that must be submitted with the proposal.

List any sources of in-kind and matching revenue, where appropriate. Plan to be flexible about your budget in case the funding organization chooses to negotiate costs.

SUPPORTING MATERIALS

Supporting materials are often placed in an appendix. These materials may endorse the project and the applicant, provide certifications, add information about project personnel and consultants, exhibit tables and charts, etc. Policies about the inclusion of supporting materials differ widely among funding organizations. Whether to allow them usually depends upon how such materials contribute to a proposal's evaluation. Restrictions are often based on excess volume, the element of bias, and relevance.

Find out if supporting materials are desired or even allowed. Be prepared to invest the time to collect resources, document capability, update a resume, collect letters, include reference reports, or do whatever is needed.

AUTHORIZED SIGNATURES

Authorized signatures are required. Proposals may be rejected for lack of an authorized signature. Be sure to allow the time to acquire a needed signature.

Tailor your proposal writing to the specifications found in the guidelines. Include no more than the number of pages allowed.

Observe the format. Is there a form to complete? Must the proposal be typed, double spaced, on $8^{1}/_{2} \times 11$-inch pages? Are cover pages allowed or desired? Caution: the beautifully bound proposal is not always appreciated or allowed. Be concise. Elaborations should add depth and scope, and not be page-fillers. Be prepared to write one or more drafts.

Submission and Follow-up

Have a submission checklist and be sure to check the final product against it. The proposal must be neat, complete, and on time, with the requested number of copies and original authorized signatures. Address the proposal as directed in the guidelines. Be sure all required documentation is included.

When a suitable period of time has elapsed, contact the funding source about the status, evaluation, and outcome of your proposal. It is important to request feedback about a proposal's strengths and weaknesses, although this information is sometimes unavailable, especially from funding organizations with a large volume of submissions. Such information may also be useful if you choose to approach the same or a different funding organization again with your idea.

Grant Information Online

The Foundation Center (www.fdncenter.org) is an independent non-profit information clearinghouse, established in 1956 to foster public understanding of the foundation field by collecting, organizing, analyzing, and disseminating information on foundations, corporate giving, and related subjects. The audiences that call on the center's resources include grant seekers, grant makers, researchers, policymakers, the media, and the general public. The Foundation Center operates libraries at five locations. These include national collections at its headquarters in New York City and at its field office in Washington, D.C., and regional collections at its offices in Atlanta, Cleveland, and San Francisco. Center libraries provide access to a unique collection of materials on philanthropy and are open to the public free of charge. Professional reference librarians are on hand to show library users how to research funding information using the center's publications and other materials and resources.

Each center-operated library offers free weekly orientations on the funding research process. These orientations are designed to give representatives of nonprofit organizations an overview of the foundation and corporate-giving universe and to introduce them to the effective use of the center's publications, resources, and services. Center staff can also tailor orientations to the specific needs and interests of various groups. To learn more about the center's orientations or to schedule a library tour, call the center-operated library nearest you.

Reference materials found at center libraries:

Forms 990-PF—Internal Revenue Service information returns are filed annually by more than forty thousand U.S. private foundations. These forms are often the only primary source of information on the many foundations that do not issue annual reports. Information provided on 990-PF forms includes fiscal data, grants awarded by a foundation, and the names of the foundation's officers and trustees.

Grant maker materials—Each library maintains an extensive collection of foundation annual reports and corporate giving reports, as well as newsletters, press releases, and application guidelines.

Directories, books, and periodicals—Foundation Center–operated libraries have available for public use multiple copies of the center's publications, in addition to hundreds of other directories, books, and periodicals on such topics as fund-raising, board relations, corporate responsibility, foundation salaries, nonprofit management, and program planning.

Foundation and nonprofit literature online—The center's bibliographic database contains listings for more than twelve thousand books and articles, many with abstracts, relating to philanthropy and the nonprofit sector.

The center also supports cooperating collections located in public libraries, community foundation offices, and other nonprofit agencies in all fifty states. Cooperating collections offer a core collection of center publications free to the public, and their staffs are trained to direct patrons to appropriate resources on funding information. Many cooperating collections also have directories and reports on local funding organizations as well as copies of IRS information returns for private foundations in their state or region. For the address and telephone number of a cooperating collection in a given location, visit the Foundation Center Web site and click on the appropriate hyperlink or call the center at 1-800-424-9836.

The Foundation Center annually issues more than sixty publications, among them directories of foundation and corporate grant makers, grants lists, research studies, bibliographies, and authored works on subjects relating to fund-raising, foundations, and non-profit management. While many center resources and services are available on a complimentary basis, for others a fee corresponding to the cost of online time or the amount of staff time required to fill a request is charged. The Foundation Center's database contains comprehensive information on more than forty thousand grant-making foundations and direct corporate-giving programs. The contents of the center's database are available to subscribers through DIALOG Information Services. Custom searches performed by center staff are conducted using DIALOG files or the center's internal database, depending on the nature of the information request.

The additional online resources listed below should also help you develop successful community networking grant proposals.

Association for Supervision and Curriculum Development (ASCD) (www.ascd.org/home.html) provides regular grant alerts, tips for writing grant proposals, ten things to do before you write a grant proposal, how to find funding, grant broker services, and other information.

Education-related Grants Information (homepage.dave-world. net/~npowell/grant.htm) includes "ten tips for grant writers," "the elements of a grant proposal," "why proposals get rejected," and "resources for grant writers."

Federal Grants Management Handbook (www.thompson.com/tpg/ fed_gts/gran/gran.html) is a two-volume handbook designed to provide practical advice and straightforward answers to help grant managers comply with complex administrative requirements for federal grants. According to the publisher, it is a comprehensive, detailed, and timely reference tool that covers regulations, executive orders, and administrative and court decisions affecting federal grants management. Your subscription includes monthly updates to the loose-leaf handbook and *Current Developments,* a newsletter with timely coverage of key issues and events. Also available are twenty-three separate "Federal Agency Reference" chapters that detail specific information about funding agencies' programs, organizational structures, and grant administration polices.

Fundsnet (www.fundsnetservices.com) is a minority-owned site and was created for the purpose of providing information on resources available on the Internet to nonprofit organizations, parents, and educators. Located in northeast Connecticut, it offers perhaps the most comprehensive directory of foundations and funding organizations available anywhere on the Internet. The site is maintained by A. Gil de Lamadrid, who conducts all research on the resources provided in this site for the benefit of visitors.

Grant Resource Center (www.worldprofit.com/native/nagrant.htm) provides hypertext links to hundreds of potential funding organizations in a variety of funding categories.

GrantsNet (www.hhs.gov/progorg/grantsnet/) is an online grant information service provided by the U.S. Department of Health and Human Services (HHS). It is a free public access computer network for finding information about HHS and other federal grant programs. It is one of the eleven networks created under the auspices of Vice President Gore's National Performance Review (NPR) (www.npr.gov/) to provide governmentwide information and resources in an online, easily accessible, and meaningful manner.

GrantsNet serves as a vehicle and catalyst for continuous improvement and innovation in federal grants management practices, policies, and information dissemination. It provides a medium for the sharing of ideas, successes, news, and lessons learned and an archival reference library of grant-related legislation, regulations, and policies. The major thrust of GrantsNet is to allow members of the public to cut through government red tape—to find the information they want when they want it and learn whom to directly contact for additional information.

Grantsmanship Center (TGCI) (www.tgci.com) provides fundraising training and information for the nonprofit sector. Since it was founded in 1972, TGCI has trained more than sixty-five thousand agency staff in grantsmanship, program planning, and fund-raising. TGCI also produces a wide range of low-cost publications, including *Program Planning and Proposal Writing*. Scores of foundation and government grant makers have adopted it as their official application format. *The Grantsmanship Center Magazine,* with a circulation of over 200,000, is distributed free of charge to staff of nonprofit organizations and government agencies. The magazine publishes authoritative articles on nonprofit administration, resource development, and grant-related issues. It also contains listings of the center's current publications and upcoming training events.

Internet Nonprofit Center (www.nonprofits.org/) includes a library of publications, information, and data about nonprofit organizations and the nonprofit sector, generally by sources other than nonprofits themselves. The Nonprofit Locator will help you find any charity in the United States.

Learning Institute for Nonprofit Organizations (www.uwex. edu/li/). The Society for Nonprofit Organizations (danenet.wicip.org/snpo/index.html), the University of Wisconsin Extension, and Television Wisconsin, Inc., support the institute in order to provide educational programs that will enable nonprofits to assume a larger role in community capacity building, coordination of services, and collaborative initiatives. The Institute uses a variety of technologies to provide nationwide access to education, information, tools, and networking volunteers at the local and national level. The Learning Institute for Nonprofit Organizations has developed an educational curriculum that focuses on the needs of nonprofit board members, volunteers, and staff members. Many of the educational offerings will be delivered as live satellite video programs.

LR Resources (www.lrr.net/grant1.htm) provides a free online resource for not-for-profit, charitable, and educational organizations. For-profit organizations and businesses may purchase this guide. Includes a "Ten-Point Plan for Standard Grant Funding Proposal" that pertains to private (rather than public, or government) grant seeking. The comprehensive grant writing guide includes a complete sample: grant application, grant budget, and cover sheet and cover letter. Also included are hyperlinks to grant makers.

National Charities Information Bureau (NCIB) (www.give.org/) was founded in 1918 to promote informed giving and charitable integrity, to enable more contributors to make sound giving decisions, and to do all it can to encourage giving to charities that need and merit support. The bureau evaluates national charitable organizations against NCIB standards.

NonProfit Times **Online** (www.nptimes.com/) provides information about and for nonprofit organizations. Each month "Ask Dr. Nonprofit" features a new expert in nonprofit management. *NonProfit Times* Online users are invited to submit questions to be answered by the guest expert.

Philanthropy and Nonprofit Resources (www.catholic.org/ neworleans/nonprofit.html) provides numerous links to pertinent online resources.

Philanthropy News Digest (fdncenter.org/phil/philmain.html) is an online publication of the Foundation Center.

Resources for Educational Grant Seekers (www.col-ed.org/fund/) provides hyperlinks to governmental and nongovernmental grant makers, nonmonetary awards and opportunities, hyperlinks or contact information related to grants-related publications, and tips for the grant seeker.

Fund-Raising Information Online

The American Fundraising Institute (www.afri.org/) offers how-to booklets (topics include *Special Events, Training and Orientation, Job Descriptions, Recruiting and Activating Volunteers, Volunteer and Staff Training*), seminars and retreats, a "turn-key plan for development," a "spark plug plan for development," capital fund-raising management, and a planned giving program.

Charity Village (www.charityvillage.com/) encourages, supports, and services Canadian charities.

Fundraising Auction Guide (www.highbidder.com/) contains information about how to conduct a successful fund-raising auction. The worksheets contained within the book (now available on floppy disk) will define your course and give you a clear pathway to achieve your goal.

Fund-Raising.Com (www.fund-raising.com/) provides a wide range of fund-raising information.

Fundraising Online (www.fundraisingonline.com) offers a free e-mail newsletter about using the Internet to raise funds.

Grassroots Fundraising (www.gil.com.au/~pnash/) offers a collection of ideas, hints, and tips to improve your next fund-raising effort.

Nonprofit Auction (www.npauction.com/) is a Web site that allows users to purchase quality items while simultaneously helping worthy causes. All the items listed on this site benefit nonprofit organizations. If your bid is the highest one when the auction closes, your dollars go to the nonprofit listed and you get a great item in return. This site is just beginning but plans to offer a wide variety of items from various nonprofit organizations. The goal is to provide users with a continuous supply of unique and interesting items to bid on.

Red Nose Comic Relief (www.fund-raising.com/comictopten.html) offers a list of the "Top Ten Wacky Fundraising Ideas."

Virtual Warehouse (www.vwh.com/fundraising/) contains a wealth of information on fund-raising and on companies that can help you plan and run a successful campaign.

➡ Good Ideas

Listed below are thoughts and suggestions passed along by my interviewees that relate to funding your community network:

- ➡ Address two major questions up front: How do you allocate the costs and how will you pay the bills?
- ➡ Establish a fund-raising committee and make its primary mission to interface with the service clubs in the community.
- ➡ Get local businesses to sponsor community network phone lines and have the bills sent directly to the sponsors. After the first year, the bill will become part of the sponsor's budget and they will continue to pay it.
- ➡ Have guaranteed funding sources in place for at least two years.
- ➡ The Tallahassee Free-Net had good luck with an auction of donated merchandise that was televised on cable TV. The local cable company donated time on one of its channels for the broadcast. The TV studio was donated by a local entertainment center and its parking lot provided the venue for a simultaneous used-computer yard sale. People attending the yard sale were able to witness the TV auction and to call in their bids

using cellular phones distributed at the site by a local cellular phone company. An "attention getter" for the events was a "computer drop." This consisted of dropping defective, obsolete computers from a fifty-foot-high cherry picker. Next time, they're going to try "computer bowling."

For More Information

Blacksburg Electronic Village: One Time and Continuous Cost Projections (Business Case Materials). (www.bev.net/project/draum/snowden/Bus_c.html)

Critical Issues in Fundraising, edited by Dwight F. Burlingame. New York: Wiley, 1997. ISBN: 0471174653.

Financial and Accounting Guide for Not-for-Profit Organizations, by Malvern J. Gross et al. 5th ed. New York: Wiley, 1995. ISBN: 0471104744.

Financial Planning for Nonprofit Organizations, by Jody Blazek. New York: Wiley, 1986. ISBN: 047112589X.

Foundation Center Guide to Funding for Information Technology. (www.fdncenter.org)

This Web site provides information for nonprofit organizations eager to enhance their services with the latest technologies. The *National Guide to Funding for Information Technology* provides facts on more than four hundred foundations and corporate direct giving programs, each with a history of awarding grant dollars to projects involving information technology.

Foundation Center Grant Guides provide up-to-date information on the grants recently awarded in various topic areas including aging; alcohol and drug abuse; arts, culture, and the humanities; children and youth; community/economic development, housing, and employment; crime, law enforcement, and abuse prevention; elementary and secondary education; environmental protection and animal welfare; film, media, and communications; foreign and international programs; health programs for children and youth; higher education; homeless; hospitals, medical care, and research; human/civil rights; libraries and information services;

literacy, reading, and adult/continuing education; matching and challenge support; medical and professional health education; mental health, addictions, and crisis services; minorities; physically and mentally disabled; program evaluation grants; public health and diseases; public policy and public affairs; recreation, sports, and athletics; religion, religious welfare, and religious education; scholarships, student aid, and loans; science and technology programs; social and political science programs; social services; and women and girls.

Foundation Resources: Community Networks, Telecenters, and Televillages, by Tim Walter. 1996. (www.aspeninst.org/rural/foundres.html)

Missouri Express Resource Guides. (outreach.missouri.edu/moexpress/guides/)

Guide 26: Developing a Financial Plan, by Ted L. Gallion

Guide 27: Funding Options, by Ted L. Gallion

National Center for Nonprofit Boards.   (www.ncnb.org)

This Web site includes publication information for a variety of booklets related to nonprofit organization management and governance, including financial management.

Public Utility Commissions and Sustainable Funding for Community Technology, by Ellis Jacobs.   (www.ctcnet.org/puco1.html)

U.S. Department of Housing and Urban Development Bookshelf 3: Communities.   (www.hud.gov/bshelf3.html)

NOTES

1. This checklist was adapted from the *HUD Neighborhood Network's Resource Guide* (www.hud.gov/nnw/nnwhowto.pdf).
2. Missouri Express Resource Guide 27, *Funding Options,* by Ted Gallion. 1997. (outreach.missouri.edu/moexpress/guides/moex27-1.html)
3. Steve Cisler, communication to the author.

7

Marketing and Public Relations

Throughout the development and implementation of your community network, you need a planned marketing campaign that is directed to your users, potential users, volunteers, and supporters. The broad goal of this campaign is to further the mission of the community network.

Joan Waldron, Chair of the Communications Committee of the Chebucto Community Network in Halifax, Nova Scotia, recommends you develop a strategic campaign. "You will need to communicate with and interact with many groups of people within the 'general public.' These groups respond in different ways and need to be considered separately." Waldron recommends you get to know your clients, communicate with them, partner with them, help them to understand how important and exciting community networks are to their future.[1]

The Marketing Process

Marketing is often confused with advertising and promotion, which are really the end steps of a comprehensive marketing plan.

Particularly since computers, online communications, and community networking are not yet commonplace in most communities, you need to consider marketing as an integral component of your program development and community education efforts. Much of what you will want to achieve involves reaching out to new individuals, new groups. This involves marketing.

Marketing is a concept that comes directly from the business world but has equal value and applicability to nonprofit organizations. In order to think about what this means for your community network, it helps to know about the "Five Ps" of marketing:

Product—the services or goods that you provide

Price—how much you charge for these services or goods

Public—to whom you want to provide your product

Place—where your products are available

Promotion—how you let your public know about your product

An excellent resource to consider is *The Marketing Workbook for Nonprofit Organizations* by Gary J. Stern, published by the Amherst H. Wilder Foundation. This book was a primary resource for much of this chapter.* If you are the person who will oversee the marketing of your community networking activities, I strongly suggest you obtain and read this book, since it goes into far greater detail than I have here.

Whether you need to market the community network overall or one particular program, there are five steps to the marketing process: (1) set marketing goals, (2) position your organization, (3) conduct a marketing audit, (4) develop a marketing plan, and (5) develop a promotional campaign.

Set Marketing Goals

When setting your marketing goals, be clear up front about what it is you want to accomplish. This will help you know how to be successful and when you have achieved success. There are two types of marketing goals: action goals and image goals. Action goals are objective, measurable accomplishments that you establish for the community

---

* Adapted from *Marketing Workbook for Nonprofit Organizations,* by Gary J. Stern, copyright 1990 Amherst H. Wilder Foundation. Used with permission. For more information on Wilder Foundation publications, call 1-800-274-6024.

network. Examples of action goals would include: number of community network subscribers, number of community organization Web pages online, number of telephone support calls answered, increase in local funding raised.

There are four questions to answer concerning your action goals:

What are the best results we could achieve and when can we expect to achieve them? You should think optimistically here. If you don't aim high, you surely won't achieve dramatic success.

What external factors might improve or detract from our ability to achieve the ideal? As a part of your thinking, be sure to consider the overall size of your community (i.e., your market size) and what percentage of that market your goals represent. For instance, getting ten businesses to sponsor phone lines might be easier in a large metropolitan area than in a small rural community.

What internal resource limitations (e.g., money, personnel, time) might affect our effort to achieve ideal results?

Given our current situation, what goals are realistic and when should they be achievable?

Image goals, on the other hand, are designed to increase awareness of the community network or its perception in the community. For instance: to be known as the online source for information about your community or as the coordinator of many organizations' efforts to improve computer and online literacy in the community.

Position Your Organization

This step is necessary if you are uncertain of your desired image or how you want the community network to be viewed by the public. This step involves establishing your unique role—your niche—in the community. In this step, you determine what it is you do that others do not do. In some communities, the role of the community network may be to coordinate and publicize the already established and ongoing work of other groups. In other communities, it may be to define, then implement, computer and online information literacy services. This presents another reason why a community assessment is so important. You do not want to reinvent the wheel or duplicate ongoing efforts.

To accomplish this step, it helps to create a "positioning statement," which is not to be confused with your mission statement (which you also need). "Your mission should define the specific outcomes your organization is after—what good you intend to do and with whom. It is a statement of accountability. Your positioning statement pinpoints the unique role you want to play in the community. It cites the specific niche you fill and, in a very few words, describes how you fill it. It is a statement of character and reputation" (Stern 1990, p. 32).

Stern recommends the following ways to establish your niche:

Make sure everyone directly connected with the community network (staff, board, volunteers) is aware of your positioning statement and understands what it means to the organization.

Regularly test and deliver your positioning statement through presentations to community groups.

Develop a public statement and use it consistently. This statement is just a paragraph blending your mission and your positioning statements.

Maintain a presence in the community.

Ensure that the media know you.

Be vocal when issues come up that affect the community network.

Form an advisory council.

Deliver. "The single most critical factor in establishing your niche is consistent delivery of your top-notch services and programs. There never has been and never will be a substitute for quality" (Stern, p. 36).

Conduct a Marketing Audit

In this step, you evaluate your current marketing efforts against the Five Ps and then decide how each "P" might be enhanced or improved. For instance:

PRODUCT

What community networking services are we providing? To what extent do these services meet our current users' needs? How satisfied are our current users with these services? Is there any aspect to these services that could be improved?

PRICE

Depending upon your community network's setup, the "price" could be money or it could be people's time and trust. In any case, the price can be set too high or too low. A well-constructed budget can be most helpful here since, in most instances, you want to cover your costs but not make much, if any, profit.

In order to fairly establish your price, you need to consider the following questions:

- How much does it actually cost the community network to deliver its service(s)?
- Do some or all of your prospective users have the means to pay the actual cost?
- Will users perceive enough value to pay what you need to charge?
- How much do others charge for similar services?
- Should you have a sliding fee scale?

PUBLIC

Develop a list of every possible public; then distinguish between your primary and secondary publics. Primary publics include the individuals and organizations who actually use the community network or refer new users or information providers to it. Secondary publics are those individuals or organizations that you will market to at some future time as well as those to keep informed of the network's progress. You should define your services according to the benefits each provides to each public group.

PLACE

Place can mean the physical location or how you distribute your services. For instance, do you maintain an office where people can drop by, learn about the community network, and receive services? Is this separate and distinct from, say, your public library? Do you offer telephone support? Is the only way to interact with the community network online?

PROMOTION

What activities, if any, are currently underway to get the word out about the community network? How effective are these activities? Do these promotional activities include a mix of online and traditional media such as radio, television, and newspapers? More information about developing an effective promotional campaign is contained later in this chapter.

Develop a Marketing Plan

The marketing plan aligns the Five Ps with the marketing goals. Then you determine what tasks are necessary to implement the plan, assign roles, create activity time lines and completion dates, and allocate available resources. When implementing the marketing plan, Stern makes the following recommendations:

- Have a clear chain of command
- Keep people updated and involved
- Keep communication flowing among all those implementing the plan
- Be flexible and responsive
- Evaluate and update regularly

Develop a Promotional Campaign

The promotional campaign includes all the methods you use to achieve your action and image goals. "An effective promotional message motivates your audience to take a specific action, and promises a desirable benefit if they do. . . . Your promotional message should specifically ask your audience to take the next step." [2]

Joan Waldron says you need to work at establishing your recognition factor right from the start and that demands a good graphic representation. "You need to be in people's faces," she says. "The way to do this is through a well-designed, eye-catching, image or logo which says your community network works wonders." Seek out the services of a professional graphic artist to create a professional look. Then use the logo on every public communication. Have business cards printed that can be spread throughout the community to let people know about the community network's existence and how to become a user. Since advertising is expensive, look for ways to partner. Waldron suggests that some of the least expensive and yet most effective promotional tools for the community network include flyers and posters, press releases, feature stories, and public service announcements (PSA). Her suggestions include:

Flyers and posters—Where to put them? How much will they cost? Who will post them and take them down? Are they effective?

Press releases—Make it a news story, not a commercial pitch. Tell readers about the uniqueness of your event and the people taking part. Figure out ahead of time how long it should be. Overwriting material makes work for editors and your chance of getting into print might be lost. Know what the deadlines are and meet them. Your press release should be professional looking. Double space with good-sized margins for editors' instructions and remarks. Dailies usually have their own photo staff but weeklies usually welcome good black and white photos. Make sure all the right people are on your contact list; keep it up to date—it's one of the most important items you'll have in your office.

Feature stories—Keep the story between two and three hundred words. It must have a local angle. Be prepared for the story to be edited. Write the story in units so that if one unit is removed it doesn't mess up the entire thing. Ideas for good news stories: exciting Web pages, communication by e-mail with a distant relative, genealogy connections, finding a "cyberpal."

Public service announcements—These are usually no more than thirty words long so you need to make every word count. If you are sending it to a weekly paper, include a longer version so it can be edited without changing the sense and the lure. Make sure all the Ws (who, what, when, where, why) are included.

Special events—Target your audience. Special events attract media attention, and we all need media attention.

Stern makes the following recommendations concerning your overall promotional efforts:

Gear the tools to the audience.

Plan how each tool can be used to the maximum effect.

Pick the right mix of techniques—within your budget.

Repeat your message frequently over an extended period of time.

If it worked, do it again.

Don't abandon the basics. That is, don't be thrown off track by success or seduced by "glitz." No matter how well things are going don't assume you've got it made. Continue attending to the basic promotional campaign.

Stay on course. Remember, most marketing is a long-term investment.

Promotional Techniques

There are many promotional techniques you might want to consider. Further details are provided in Stern's *Marketing Workbook for Nonprofit Organizations.*

Advertising	News release
Annual report	Personal sales
Attitude	Poster
Billboard	Presentation
Brochure	Publication
Direct mail	Public service announcement
Editorial	Special events
Endorsement	Specialty items: mouse pads, t-shirts
Feature story	Talk shows: radio and television
Letters to the editor	Telethon/telemarketing
Logo/visual identity	Trade shows
Networking	Video
News conference	Word of mouth
Newsletter	

Remember the following points concerning your overall marketing efforts:

Marketing is a sustained effort. You need to evaluate your progress regularly. Be flexible as necessary and respond promptly to needed changes.

Involve the right people. You need to be sure that all those involved—board members, staff, volunteers—know about and are involved with your marketing efforts. People in leadership positions should, at minimum, be involved in decisions related to goals and positioning. People in management and staff positions should, at minimum, be involved in decisions that affect day-to-day operations.

Make sure that the organization is committed to devoting the necessary resources to complete the marketing plan. There is no point in developing a comprehensive plan if none of its activities can be implemented.

As part of your marketing planning activities, you need to consider whether you will have enough capacity to meet the demand for your services. Performing a scenario or "What if?" analysis is very helpful as a reality check on your activities. For instance:

> What if our promotion succeeds beyond our expectations? Will we be able to give an account to everyone who calls or develop Web pages for every nonprofit organization that is interested?

> What if we get all the grants for which we have applied? Will we be able to gear up fast enough to keep our promises? Will we be able to support our grant project partners in the form and manner we agreed to do?

> What if it takes a year (or more) to build up demand for our community networking services? Can we afford the lean months? Can we afford it if our projections prove too optimistic? Too pessimistic?

While you should be optimistic about your marketing plans, activities, and the results you can achieve with a well-executed campaign, it is critical that you be realistic about your capabilities to deliver as well. Leaving your public with unrealized expectations is something you clearly want to avoid.

↦ Good Ideas

Listed below are thoughts and suggestions passed along by my interviewees that relate to community network marketing and public relations:

- ↦ Always try to figure out what the "newsy" angle is.
- ↦ At least quarterly, do something special to get the word out about the community network.
- ↦ Do a special targeted mailing to the churches in the community, telling about the availability of Web sites and orientation sessions.

➤ Establish a PR budget and see to it that those in charge follow through.

➤ Library-focused strategic planning can be a valuable tool not only for redefining how you deliver library services but for marketing the community network and its association with the library to the public.

➤ Make sure that all the organizations that are a part of the community network continue over time to promote its activities.

➤ Ongoing PR activities: speakers bureau, news releases about training classes.

➤ Publicize all of the library's programs online through the community network.

➤ Publicize the community network through other organizations' newsletters. Working through these organizations is key —let them help you get the word out.

➤ Put someone in charge of community relations.

➤ Put your URL on everything you do.

➤ The community network gives people another reason to visit the library—it is another product that the library offers. When you add another product to your line, it will bring more people in. Don't judge why people come into the library—as long as they come.

➤ Volunteers help to spread the word to new clienteles: students, senior citizens, human services people, techies.

➤ Work with the local public utilities or tax commission to include a bookmark about the community network in their next broad mailing.

For More Information

The Board's Role in Public Relations and Communications, by Joyce L. Fitzpatrick. Washington, D.C.: National Center for Nonprofit Boards, 1992. (www.ncnb.org)

Missouri Express Resource Guides.
(outreach.missouri.edu/moexpress/guides/)

Guide 19: Communicating to Build Support for Your Community Network, by Sandy Stegall

NOTES

1. Joan Waldron, "Internal Communications and External Public Relations" (paper presented at the Telecommunications Canada Conference, Halifax, Nova Scotia, Canada, August 1997). Used with permission.

2. Ibid. Used with permission.

8

Developing Local Online Information

Providing online access to local information is a critical function for most community networks. The community network manages a file server, which has a dedicated connection to the Internet. Increasingly the file server is actually a Web server—meaning the local information will (1) be multimedia (chiefly text and graphics), (2) contain "hypertext" links to similar, related materials found elsewhere on the Internet, and (3) be created using a language called HTML (hypertext markup language).

As described by Ted MacDonald in the Missouri Express Resource Guide *Developing the Community Information Store,* several issues are involved:

Identification of a Web server and provision of necessary associated activities such as regular back-up, security, and maintenance

Design of a template format for the consistent presentation of information about the community

Developing procedures for transfer and regular updating of information from community information providers to the Web server

Providing training for community information providers and those in the community who will be developing community information and Web pages[1]

Library involvement with this aspect of community networking is particularly important since librarians have special expertise in organizing materials for easy retrieval.

Delivering Local Content

Two of the Missouri Express Resource Guides provide helpful information about how to develop the local information database:

Guide 15: Deciding What Is Worthy Community Information,
by Jack D. Timmons

Guide 16: Developing the Community Information Store,
by Ted MacDonald

Montgomery-Floyd Regional Library, a partner in the Blacksburg Electronic Village, provides Web server space to organizations that meet the following criteria. Participating organizations must be non-profit, civic and civil in nature (in the public interest, pertaining to the general public), serve the people of the local geographic region, and be located within that region. They must also agree to abide by the network's acceptable use policy and keep their organization's information and graphics under two megabytes. Participating organizations may announce events and fund-raisers but may not sell merchandise or services online or list prices. Promotions or advertisements for profit-making organizations are not allowed. These requirements seem reasonable and are, in fact, typical of most community networks.

Participating nonprofits are required to have the following access capabilities, enabling them to add to or modify their information online at any time:

- A computer with full Internet access—either Mac or PC platform
- An e-mail account
- FTP (File Transfer Protocol) to upload files to the server

- A Web browser, such as Netscape or Internet Explorer, to view the files created
- Ability to create an HTML document and FTP it to the server

In return, Montgomery-Floyd Regional Library offers community organizations:

- Visibility to the entire community (and the rest of the world) via the Web
- Total control over content and the ability to update information
- Up to two megabytes of storage space on its Web server
- FTP access to the organization's own secure folder and password
- Regular tape backups of all server data
- Training on creating HTML documents and sending FTP files to the Web server
- Distribution of several shareware HTML editors
- One-day checkout of a digital camera to take high resolution digital images and limited assistance converting and posting images from the camera to the Web page

The library does not create Web pages for the nonprofits but suggests other options for organizations that cannot or do not want to do it themselves:

- Have someone capable of writing HTML volunteer to create pages for the organization
- Contract with (pay) someone to create pages for the organization
- Contract with a company to create and maintain page(s). This information could reside either on the library server or on the company's server.

Regardless of who actually creates the Web pages, good design is essential to providing local information and doing it well. Two excellent online resources for you to consider are

Yale University's Center for Advanced Instructional Media Web Guide   (info.med.yale.edu/caim/manual/index.html)

Sun Microsystem's Guide to Web Style
(www.sun. com/styleguide/)

Susan Holmes, director of the Three Rivers Free-Net (TRFN) at the Carnegie Library of Pittsburgh, feels that librarian support for TRFN's information providers is what makes TRFN successful. As she says, "We are librarians. We have experience meeting the informational needs of our customers, we know how to conduct a reference interview (for the purpose of helping information providers identify what to include in a Web site) and we are able to organize information in a way that can be understood by a broad and varied community." [2]

Holmes offers the following recommendations:

Design a template for use at the bottom of all Web pages hosted on your community network. This template produces easily navigable sites with information in the same place on each home page you host. "As librarians we know how crucial the need is for date of last update, maintainer name, and e-mail address. Also, it is important to include links back to the community network's subject pages (from which they may have come) and to outside search engines."

Give information providers a counter on their home pages so that they have an opportunity to keep track of visits for funding purposes.

The goal should be to get users into your subject guide as often as possible. TRFN does this as often as possible within its site: from the "new links" and "timely links" pages in the "What's New?" Section and from the button bar on the web page template.

Encourage information providers to create links to other local organizations that may provide next-step or complementary services in their service area or field. This local linking will create a one-stop shopping approach and easy access to information without requiring users to start from scratch with each inquiry.

Encourage simple pages. Remember that "content is king!" Encourage your information providers to check out other sites and to notice that glitz does not often produce information-rich sites.

TRFN has a "Did you know?" question of the week, month, etc., as appropriate. It has informational pages on newsmakers, recent

Nobel prize winners, and timely local topics to help users gather information about current events.

Provide training sessions for the information providers or volunteers who need more direction. TRFN training sessions include a weekly workshop where trainers are available for questions. This has resulted in many more information providers getting their pages up quickly and feeling comfortable with the process.

Give volunteers the opportunity to work with information providers after completing several community networking tasks. At TRFN, these liaisons have increased the communication of the wonderful services available in their area and have often given the information provider organization a new, devoted friend.

For Hilbert Levitz and others involved with starting the Tallahassee Free-Net in 1992, the mission with respect to local information became that of promoting a large, distributed base of local information—not necessarily residing exclusively on the Free-Net system. Tallahassee Free-Net was also designed to be a demonstration vehicle for inducing the stronger local organizations, such as local government and the hospitals, to establish servers of their own. As a consequence of this early decision, Tallahassee now has a Web presence for its local government, businesses, and nonprofit agencies that exceeds that of most cities.

Partnership has also been an important development strategy for the Tallahassee Free-Net. In one instance it mediated a partnership between various umbrella agencies and Florida State University instructors whereby students would create Web pages for local nonprofit organizations as part of their course work. For Levitz, the founder of Tallahassee Free-Net, the most successful partnership occurred with the Tallahassee Arts Council. "The Executive Director of that organization was solidly behind the project and, as a result, full suites of Web pages were created for fifty-three local arts agencies. This effort, together with pages created independently of the project, brought the Free-Net's menu for arts and cultural resources to sixty-seven entries." Similar partnerships were instituted with the United Way and with the Big Bend Environmental Forum. Although the degree of cooperation by these umbrella organizations was less than that of the arts council, these partnerships also substantially raised the number of local nonprofit organizations providing online information.

A critical element in the success of the Tallahassee partnerships was a demonstration given each semester to the group of potential client organizations. By showing what other agencies had already done, and by giving participants an opportunity to interact with one another, this demonstration reinforced cooperation between the student teams and client agencies. After the first semester the demonstrations were dropped, but the level of cooperation was found to be reduced, so the demonstrations were reinstated in subsequent semesters.

The Westplex Information Network (WIN) (www.win.org/) added a "Community Calendar" for residents to access information about events that are relevant to its service area: St. Charles County Missouri. WIN was established by the City of St. Peters, the St. Charles City-County Library District, St. Charles County Community College, St. Charles County Government, and the St. Peters Fire Protection District. The goal of the community calendar is to contain event information that promotes goodwill, betters the community, and contributes to the economic development of St. Charles County. It is expected that WIN subscribers will use the community calendar to obtain information about group or organization meetings, counseling services, softball leagues, health seminars, home-buying seminars, family events, and more. Approved WIN account holders will have the privilege of posting information about events by local organizations or businesses in support of St. Charles County residents to the community calendar. Not-for-profit organizations may elect one individual to be the information provider to WIN. Individuals and commercial businesses must submit the event information for review and approval by WIN. Information that complies with the WIN Agreement, Acceptable Use Policy, and Community Information Policies and Guidelines will be posted in a timely manner.

A similar project is underway at the Columbia Online Information Network (COIN) (www.coin.missouri.edu). COIN users access a monthly calendar from the COIN Web site. The highlighted days include posted events. Users simply highlight the date, press return (or click on it) to find out about the event(s) for that date. Future events are accessible by choosing the month you would like to see. You can also search for an event. Nonprofit groups may request that their events be added to this calendar. COIN also provides hypertext access to other local organizations' online calendars.

LapeerNet (www.lapeer.lib.mi.us), based in Lapeer County, Michigan, exemplifies how a community network can spearhead the development of local online information that garners widespread interest and enthusiasm. "Building Virtual Museums: The Art of Creating Rich Curricular Experiences and Archives on the Internet" began as a yearlong project for the whole Greater Thumb community. Lapeer County students, teachers, and librarians worked together to build meaningful, appropriate, and accurate information relevant to the K–12 community.

The central focus of the project was the Marguerite deAngeli Collection owned by Lapeer County Library. This rich archive of primary source information includes manuscripts, original illustrations, awards, family photographs, and personal correspondence and provides the opportunity to bring to life one of the most-loved twentieth-century contributors to children's literature. The family of Mrs. deAngeli, who was born and raised in Lapeer, chose to give a major portion of her life's work to the Lapeer County Library for posterity. This project makes the Marguerite deAngeli Collection available to the world through the creation of a virtual museum. The schools, meanwhile, initiated a program to train interested students in Web design and maintenance so that they could develop LapeerNet home pages for nonprofit organizations from the community.

Similar activities occur through the Willard Public Library in Battle Creek, Michigan. The library has worked to mount the collections of Kellogg Community College, the Battle Creek Art Center, and Kingman Museum of Natural History on its catalog server. Willard has had an active technology program since 1992 when the library automated access to its card catalog. After successfully transferring bibliographic records of the library's holdings, provision of community information on that catalog became a top priority. The library immediately sponsored a newspaper indexing project that mounted over twenty years worth of a library-created index to local information on the system, and that project continues with daily indexing of the paper.

In addition to the newspaper index, Willard has actively supported the collection and dissemination of other types of local history material. The Local History Collection at Willard was officially started in 1969, but in 1995 it was greatly expanded. Persons interested in the history of the area regularly meet to share in the library's resources. Efforts are underway to digitize much of the collection, which will ultimately reside on the library's Web server, making it much more widely accessible. In collaboration with the local Volunteer and Information Service Bureau, the library has mounted a community organizations file, listing hundreds of local organizations with meeting times, contact persons, and other information about the organizations. All of that community information is keyword searchable.

Many community network administrators echo the experience of the Boulder Community Network (bcn.boulder.co.us/) in that nonprofit agencies are, more often than not, likely to expect a great deal of support from community network staff and volunteers. Even human service agencies with information systems support staff find community network staff more helpful. Keep in mind that just because people understand computers and databases does not necessarily mean they can lead an agency or organization through the ins and outs of the new Internet technologies. The bottom line: organizations vary in their commitment of staff to community network activities. Their own time and goal constraints, as well as technical abilities and orientations, also limit the degree to which they can act as intermediaries for their own clientele.

Building Relationships with United Way Agencies

Most communities have found it helpful to work with the local United Way: as a potential source of funding for the community network and as a conduit to many of the nonprofit human services agencies in the community. If you want to develop a relationship with your local United Way (www.unitedway.org/), it is best to begin by setting up an informational meeting to explain the community network's mission, what needs it fulfills, and whom you serve in the community. At the same time you can find out about the United Way and the array of resources (such as professional development, management assistance, funding, and volunteer recruitment) that many local United Ways have to assist nonprofit organizations and support requirements.[3]

Meet with a member of the United Way staff, including those in positions involved in community initiatives, community problem solving, planning, allocations, fund distribution, agency relations, or community services. The name of the pertinent department varies from United Way to United Way. Bring your business plan, annual report, brochure, and other information to the meeting.

Most local United Ways have an annual fund-raising cycle for raising and distributing funds. Frequently the fund-raising campaign is in the fall with the funds being allocated in the winter or spring. Additionally, the funding priorities that drive allocations are usually set five to six months before the fund-raising campaign kicks off. So it may take a while for the community network to be considered, especially if computer literacy is a new priority (or not a priority) for your United Way.

Member agency status is the most prevalent arrangement by which a United Way provides ongoing financial and technical assistance to a nonprofit organization. To be a member agency, a nonprofit generally must have 501(c)3 status, a functioning board, a paid director, a budget, financial and programmatic accountability, fund-raising plans, an office and a phone, and a one- or two-year track record of success. If the community network does not meet these criteria, the United Way may help you move toward these goals. Unfortunately, some United Ways have been unable to reach their own fund-raising goals in recent years and, therefore, have not been able to take on new members.

Member agencies must abide by restrictions set by the local United Way. These restrictions are generally centered on the time of year that active fund-raising can take place and from whom funds can be sought.

A number of United Ways are changing the way they look at membership. Consequently several forms of affiliation are emerging for nonprofit organizations. Since each United Way is unique, the following represent examples. Other forms of affiliation may exist in your community.

Donor choice/affiliate status—Donors in many areas have expressed their desire to have more say about where their money goes. Therefore, they designate the organization(s) to which they want their United Way contributions to go. Any 501(c)3 organization in a community is eligible to receive funds through donor choice. The size of the United Way contribution is determined by the amount specified by the donors.

Priority grants—A number of United Ways engage in extensive community needs assessments from which they identify a specific group of critical community needs. The identified community needs then become the basis from which the United Way makes multiyear funding decisions.

Venture or demonstration/development grant funding—Organizations can often apply for a small grant to undertake a specific project. These grants enable the United Way to work with non-member organizations and are sometimes an entry point into more permanent funding.

Many United Ways provide support services to nonprofits in the community, regardless of whether an organization is a member of the United Way. In addition to, or instead of, base funding, the community network may be able to partake in the services offered. Not every United Way offers all of these, but it is worth finding out.

Formal and informal volunteer referral—Many United Ways support community-wide volunteer recruitment campaigns, and refer interested volunteers to nonprofit organizations. This may be carried out by a Voluntary Action Center or Volunteer Center (the name varies), which is often a division or agency of United Way. By registering the community network with the center you may be able to get volunteers to serve on your board or to help deliver the network's online information services.

Training—United Ways offer training to nonprofits on a variety of topics, including board development, long-range and strategic planning, fund-raising, and budgeting, to name a few.

Management assistance program (MAP)—Loaned executives and specialists in such areas as accounting, planning, computer programming, and personnel are often available to assist nonprofit organizations through a local United Way's Management Assistance Program. This program matches organizations that express a need in a particular area with a volunteer who has the needed expertise.

Linkages to other organizations—United Ways encourage the full utilization and integration of agency services within the community. Furthermore, United Ways sometimes broker services, which could enhance the services offered by the community network.

Executive director coalitions—In some communities, coalitions of executive directors of United Way organizations exist to provide opportunities to network, learn new skills, and work together on issues that affect nonprofit organizations.

In-kind services—Such services might include printing, office space, or administrative support.

Gifts-in-kind America—Businesses donate such materials as computer hardware and software, books, vacuum cleaners, office supplies, and furniture. Additionally, some local United Ways are also securing donated building supplies. The businesses often make the materials available to local United Ways and nonprofit organizations for the cost of shipping. Make your wish list known to the United Way in the event that these items become available.

Work at fostering a reciprocal relationship with your United Way. There is a trend among United Ways across the country to pursue diversity on their boards of governors as well as on the volunteer committees established by their boards. Many United Ways may need help finding appropriate community leaders to fill these spots. Your recommendations of volunteers to serve on United Way committees could be quite useful to your United Way and to strengthening your working relationship.

Information and Referral

Information and referral (I&R) is a service that helps people in need find the services that can best alleviate or eliminate that need. The main functions of an I&R agency are to

develop and update files about community resources in the human service area

provide information about these resources and make formal referrals to the appropriate service agencies

follow up with clients and service agencies to determine if the needed service was obtained and if it adequately met the need

participate in community education activities

engage in advocacy for the development of new human services

prepare statistical reports on service requests and undertake research on local needs to help community planners and funding agencies

The Alliance of Information and Referral Systems (AIRS) (www. airs.org), the professional I&R association, traces its beginnings to the late 1960s. The first I&R discussions were sponsored by what later became United Way of America.

By the early 1970s, I&R services were proliferating in all parts of the United States and Canada. Local and federal funds became available to a variety of human service systems for starting and operating I&R programs. Agencies serving the handicapped, the aged, and the economically disadvantaged became more involved in providing I&R services. It was clear that the fast-developing field of I&R required a broad collective effort aimed at improving the quality of I&R delivery in every setting. AIRS was incorporated in 1973 as a focal point for the I&R field and to work in the public interest for improved access to services. It has increasingly attracted diverse individuals and organizational members worldwide.[4]

AIRS has five main goals: (1) to be known and respected nationally as representing the field of I&R through the development of quality standards and methods of evaluating I&R services and through networking with related national organizations; (2) to educate the public about the nature and purpose of I&R and to promote I&R on a national level; (3) to produce publications that will serve the needs of the I&R field, such as the national directory, newsletter, and journal; (4) to provide technical assistance to AIRS members through the development of a national clearinghouse on I&R, including a bibliographic database, skills bank, and sample materials from I&R agencies; and (5) to recognize involvement and accomplishments in the I&R field, through annual awards as well as through special recognition of members in the AIRS directory.

I&R on the Internet

Information and Referral Resource Network (www.ir-net.com/) is an online directory that lists agencies throughout the United States that provide human services to the public. A wide variety of services are represented, including information and referral, social service, case management, health care, counseling, mental health, day care, educational, employment, domestic violence, recreation, substance abuse, and welfare programs. Some of the I&R services with an established presence on the Web include:

JEONET Iowa City / Coralville Community Index, Iowa City, Iowa
(www.jeonet.com/city/citindex.htm)

Community Information and Referral Service, Phoenix, Arizona
(www.cirs.org/)

Arroyo Verdugo Communities Information, Los Angeles,
California   (www.cwire.com/orgs/index.html)

Prairienet Community Network, Champaign, Illinois
(www.prairienet.org/)

The Kansas State Library has spearheaded a local effort to create
the Community Library Organizations Union Database (CLOUD)
(skyways.lib.ks.us/kansas/community/about_cloud.html). This online service is intended to advance I&R by creating links to not-
for-profit programs of service including human, social, civic, governmental, educational, and recreational programs. CLOUD is unique in
that it is a statewide project and does not represent the interests of any
single information and referral entity.

CLOUD is a merged, online database of community information
resources that serves the information and referral needs of users, represents communities throughout Kansas, has a consistent format and
makes consistent use of names and subject headings, has an easy-to-
use yet powerful interface, is regularly updated and maintained, and
delivers information to as many Kansas libraries, agencies, and residents as possible.

Cataloging Community Information

An interesting and innovative project is currently underway at
SOLINET, the Southeast Library Network. The goals of the Online
Integrated Communities Information Systems Project (www.
solinet.net/monticello) are to improve access to electronic public
information by applying standards to support information sharing
and interoperability in five southeastern communities. The project
supports regional sharing of public information, improves infrastructure and technical capacity, provides documented models for other
communities, and includes an empowerment evaluation process. The
community networks will apply MARC CIF and GILS to their public
information databases in a Z39.50 compliant environment.

SOLINET and its partners have been working since 1993 on the Monticello Project, to make information more accessible in the region through cooperative organization of the decentralized resources created for and distributed on the Internet. In 1996, a system and methodology were established to link and provide access to regional resources in the areas of state government economic information and library special collections. The system is functional and has been used throughout the region, but an obstacle has been discovered that currently limits growth and community involvement: most creators/distributors of electronic information have not fully employed standards in their systems.

These organizations either do not recognize the value of standards in broadening and simplifying access to electronic information or do not have the skills to implement them. There is also sometimes a lack of awareness that others beyond an obvious geographic or political boundary could find value in the information, and that other communities may have valuable information that could be shared. In addition, there is a widespread assumption that technology will somehow automatically solve these problems in the future. However, the solution in fact requires collaboration in the application of standards across communities. Even where the value of standards is acknowledged, interpretation and application are not always consistent. Consensus is needed across communities on the basic data elements to be used from various formats in order to link information across networks.

GILS (Government Information Locator Service), MARC CIF (Community Information Format), Dublin Core, and other standards define tagging and identification structures for public information resources. However, in application, there is no standardization across jurisdictions. Although the costs associated with and the technical capacity needed for implementing standards can be daunting, achieving standardization in application is critical to successful information sharing and retrieval. While SOLINET and its partners have made some progress in this area, much work needs to be done at all levels: local, state, regional, and national. Through further development of its test system, and careful work over the next two years with five communities in the Southeast, SOLINET and its partners intend to demonstrate the value of applied standards in order to provide widespread, uniform access to critical public information resources at the local and regional levels.

Providing successful access to public information resources requires cooperation among many agencies. Agencies in the project include local, county, and state government agencies; educational institutions (universities, colleges, community and technical colleges, K–12 school systems, adult education programs, etc.); business organizations (such as chambers of commerce); and public library systems. Community networks will leverage the work accomplished to date in linking decentralized information resources from state government agencies and in building interstate coordination of electronic resources. This project will continue to facilitate work with relevant state and regional agencies in order to assist in enhancing the information resources made available through community networks, as well as ensuring standardization and interoperability.

The project is centered in each community at a local library, providing a means for coordination as well as an outlet for information distribution that is accessible to all in the community. Libraries, especially public libraries, have traditionally maintained local information referral files to connect end users to community services. Many of these files are still paper-based; however, some communities have begun to convert them to electronic formats. As traditional sources of information itself and of systems for information access, libraries and librarians are critical components of any community network.

Linking information from the local communities at the state and regional level allows for important sharing of resources. Information from local communities can be compiled to assist in city, county, and state governance. Citizens can find information on distant communities when considering a move. Students can learn about the history, industry, culture, and resources of different communities, and can retrieve information to enable comparative study.

Business and industry can collect information to assist them in growth and development, identifying and approaching new markets for services. No matter what their purpose or location, individuals will be able to find information throughout the regional system via similar search processes. This will simplify search and retrieval for users. At the same time, SOLINET's work with libraries to make local public information resources accessible through the information infrastructure will have an immediate and positive impact on local communities.

The project will provide a model for all communities and groups seeking to make data available though the information infrastructure. With existing standards and technology used consistently, information will become easier to access in local communities and across the nation. The model will show how valuable and necessary standards are in the creation and distribution of information and will guide other communities' projects. Standards will also ease maintenance of systems and electronic information resources, and will ensure interoperability.

➻ Good Ideas

Listed below are thoughts and suggestions passed along by my interviewees that relate to developing local online information:

- ➻ Balance the informative with the whimsical.
- ➻ Encourage your information providers to be users of the community network as well.
- ➻ Even if you can't find any partners, put up a home page with links to the right places. Service is not nearly as important as the content.
- ➻ Go back to basic principles: the patron, the question, and helping the patron answer the question. Don't think of the format.
- ➻ Have each special collection within the library develop its own home page. Then let the librarian in charge do whatever he or she wants with the page.
- ➻ Have reference librarians check for outdated links during down time while they are working the desk.
- ➻ Keep the content family oriented and retain control over users' postings. Since everyone is concerned about pornographic content online, keeping this focus is very helpful when approaching businesses and government.
- ➻ Let library staff know of the potential time commitment up front—and do what you can to enable them to fold online content development into their ongoing duties.
- ➻ Let the librarian become the deal maker developing online content. Perhaps this is the future of collection development?
- ➻ Librarians are nonthreatening, not in direct competition with those unwilling to share information. Also, librarians are very curious: we always get excited by finding the answer to a

question. This makes a natural environment for helping people find information online.

↠ Local content is so important! While the "look and feel" of Web pages are important attributes to consider, the value of the online content is of paramount importance.

↠ Offer to publish the minutes of local government meetings online; this can be a potential source of income for the community network.

↠ Providing content online means repackaging information. Scout actively and then repackage what you find into a user-friendly format. Consider it collection development: before, it was on paper; now it is electronic, too.

↠ Recruit people with some familiarity, interest, or expertise with the content area so they can recognize the reputable and useful new sites to add.

↠ Recruit two SIG (special interest group) monitors for each content area.

↠ Schedule regular training sessions for information providers to ensure they do things "properly."

↠ Securing local government information is the most difficult task. To do so you must establish a personal rapport: not with an agency but person-to-person. Otherwise, they don't care. It is a tender relationship that must be cultivated daily. Let people know you can get them the information they need.

↠ Serve as a liaison between the academic community and the community at large. Do this by subscribing to pertinent discussion lists, interfacing with faculty, etc.

↠ Start out small—don't have a lot of "links to nowhere."

↠ The lower you go in the organization, the more proprietary people are about the data they oversee. You need to seek out and secure broad organizational support and encouragement for data sharing.

↠ The way to get information providers to take ownership of the process is to describe the activity for them and how much time it will take. Then it does not seem so overwhelming to them. You need to make them realize it is not about putting stuff on the community network but about showing people what is available out there.

➵ Web pages that contain useful information get used a lot—which is very gratifying to the librarians who create them.

➵ Web publishing workshops specifically for nonprofit agencies are a good way to add local content easily to your Web site. Give the potential information providers a half-day HTML workshop; the result of their participation should be the beginnings of their Web page.

➵ While it is initially time-consuming to catalog all of the library's resources for inclusion on the Web site, after the initial task is complete it is easy to add new resources as they become available online.

➵ Work through your regional library council to coordinate the member libraries' involvement in and development of local online information.

➵ You'll be surprised how much e-mail you get from people thanking you for creating a particular Web page, for putting the information together. Getting recognition from people all over is very reinforcing.

For More Information

AIRS/Info Line Taxonomy.

According to AIRS, this taxonomy sets a new standard for defining services and indexing the wide variety of human services available in communities across North America. Offering 4,300 terms and 2,000 "use" references, the *Taxonomy* is the most comprehensive document of its kind. Created by Info Line of Los Angeles for its own use, the *Taxonomy* is suitable for organizations nationwide. Further information is available from Info Line, P.O. Box 4307, El Monte, CA 91734.

Making the Net Work: Online Strategies for Community-Based Organizations, by Terry Grunwald. Raleigh, N.C.: NCExchange, 1996.

One major hurdle you will probably have to face is that many of the organizations that you want to provide information will have little or no previous experience with online communications. This guide is a very helpful resource in this regard. It is unique in that it does not focus on the technology per se but addresses instead the more important issues: Why should nonprofit agencies go online? How will nonprofits use networking in day-to-day work? Is going online the right step for a particular organization? Further information about this book is available by phone: 919/856-2176; e-mail: info@ncexchange.org; or through the NCExchange Web site: www.ncexchange.org.

Missouri Express Resource Guides. (outreach.missouri.edu/moexpress/guides/)

> *Guide 15: Deciding What Is Worthy Community Information,* by Jack D. Timmons

> *Guide 16: Developing the Community Information Store,* by Ted MacDonald

Suggestions for Building Relationships with Your United Way, HUD Neighborhood Networks Partnership Report: March 26, 1997. (www.hud.gov/nnw/nnwpart1.pdf)

NOTES

1. *Missouri Express Resource Guide 16: Developing the Community Information Store,* by Ted MacDonald.
2. Susan Holmes, communication to the author.
3. Material in this section is adapted from Suggestions for Building Relationships with Your United Way, HUD Neighborhood Networks Partnership Report: March 26, 1997. (www.hud.gov/nnw/nnwpart1.pdf)
4. Further information about AIRS is available online (www.airs.org) or by contacting the AIRS National Office, P.O. Box 3546, Joliet, IL 60434. Phone: 815/744-6922.

Public Access, Training, and Technical Support

One of the most important aspects to consider when developing a community network is how to ensure equitable, convenient access to the online information services and to ensure that all citizens know how to access these resources and services effectively. Public access workstations are important, first and foremost, to the large segment of the population without personal access to a computer at home, work, or school. Also, people with personal access still often need to tap into online information from other locations. An integral component to public access is the provision of training and technical support services so that the public has the skills necessary to take maximum advantage of the resources and services that the community network makes available.

There are a number of resources to assist you with planning and implementing public access workstations. The federal Department of Housing and Urban Development (HUD) (www.hud.gov/nnw/ nnwindex.html) has funding available for establishing a Neighborhood Networks Center (NNC). An NNC is a facility where computers are available to residents of multifamily apartment buildings for job-related, educational, and other community-based purposes. The unique feature of an NNC is that residents can and do participate in the planning and creation of the NNC, its growth and operations.

HUD permits these funds to be spent on computer hardware and software, distance learning equipment, securing and retrofitting usable space, and staff salaries.

Full details about the NNC Project are contained in a 350-page Resource Guide, which is available online in portable document format (PDF) (www.hud.gov/nnw/nnwhowto.pdf). Free software that enables you to download and read or print PDF documents, Adobe Acrobat, may be downloaded from Adobe Corporation (www.adobe.com). The resource guide, in addition to numerous other materials available at the HUD Web site, offers a wealth of useful information regardless of where you plan to develop public access workstations.

Another organization to investigate is the Community Technology Centers' Network (CTCNet) (www.ctcnet.org/). CTCNet's broad goal is to bring together agencies and programs that provide opportunities for people of all ages to learn about and use computers and related technologies. For a modest fee, your community network (or library) can become a CTCNet affiliate. In return you will be linked to others who have the experience and the expertise to help you deliver effective public access services.

Even if you do not choose to affiliate, CTCNet provides an excellent *Community Technology Center Start-Up Manual,* which is available free online or in print for $25. Topics covered in this manual include: time line and process; mapping community resources; determining program focus; staffing; software selection and criteria; space, hardware, and security; scheduling, outreach, and self-assessment; and budgeting and funding.

On a broader scale, CTCNet shares with Playing to Win, its founding organization, a recognition that, in an increasingly technologically dominated society, people who are socially or economically disadvantaged will become further disadvantaged if they lack access to computers and computer-related technologies. CTCNet envisions a society in which all people are equitably empowered by technology skills and usage. As a leading advocate of equitable access to computers and related technologies, CTCNet invites, initiates, and actively encourages partnerships and collaborations with other individuals and organizations that offer resources in support of its mission.

Local Places, Global Connections: Libraries in the Digital Age, a report published by Libraries for the Future (LFF) and the Benton Foundation in 1997, profiles a variety of library-sponsored community connectivity projects that can serve as prototypes for service delivery in your community.[1] The Benton Foundation and Libraries for the Future share a belief in libraries as vital community institutions in the digital age. These organizations believe that libraries can bring a focus and organization to the often bewildering and ever expanding universe of information and counter the centrifugal forces of modern life by nurturing community, civic engagement, and democratic traditions.

Local Places, Global Connections profiles eight community connectivity projects that demonstrate the potential of the public library to provide innovative, locally centered technology programs. Based largely on interviews with librarians, community organizers, and library users, the profiles offer a unique insight into the value of public access to technology. This group is representative of the many ways libraries have approached the challenge of providing electronic access to information.

While it is impossible to reflect the entire breadth and scope of programs in place throughout the country, the libraries profiled represent all regions of the United States and include state library systems as well as city systems and even individual libraries. Some of the libraries serve large urban populations while others are in rural areas. The diversity reveals the public library's tremendous potential as an institution to meet the information needs of the twenty-first century. While this report focuses primarily on public libraries, *Local Places, Global Connections* demonstrates how networked information makes all types of libraries more interdependent.

Public Access Profiles

This section describes several community networking projects underway across the United States and Canada aimed primarily at providing public access to online information resources and the Internet. These profiles are included to inspire and encourage you to move ahead with public access in your community and to recognize a small portion of the many, many communities that are changing the lives of their residents in positive ways with electronic communications.

Cape Breton, Nova Scotia, Canada (highlander.cbnet.ns.ca/cbnet/comucntr/cap). Entrepreneurs in Glace Bay, Nova Scotia, are expanding their skills and their businesses at the town's Community Access Program (CAP) site. The Cape Breton YMCA Enterprise Center

sponsors and houses the CAP facility. Experienced and novice entrepreneurs follow the center's curriculum of business courses and,
through the CAP site, learn how the world of computers and information networks can benefit them. Four CAP computers support the
center's overall training program. During the work day, site staff
reserve the computers for training and for business people who
started their companies with the assistance of the center. Other users,
such as students and residents, pay $1 per half hour to go online out-
side of training time. Center staff make a point of hiring students with
a combination of business, marketing, and technology skills. One of
these students was so successful that she now has a permanent position as the center's business review officer. High school co-op students
work at the center during their placement program. The students
benefit from the work experience and CAP site users benefit from
their involvement. Diligence in the search for reliable and committed
volunteers for the CAP site has paid off, and it is now open for an
impressive number of hours each week.

Gaspé Peninsula, Quebec, Canada (www.imagine-mms.com/
villes/saint-elzear/main.htm). The CAP site in Saint-Elzéar, Quebec,
on the Gaspé Peninsula, shows the value of the Internet to young people in outlying communities. The CAP site features a local area network of sixteen computers and ten Internet accounts in the
elementary school. Volunteer instructors work with groups of students outside regular school hours, often bringing in guest speakers to
share their knowledge. Members of the general public also receive
training. "The project brings tremendous benefit to the community,
particularly to our young people," says Denis Arsenault, Saint-Elzéar's
mayor. "It also contributes to economic development by letting us
promote the town far afield."

Two very promising partnerships grew out of the CAP project.
The town and the telephone company set up teleconferencing and
distance-education facilities for forestry courses that will be broadcast
from the local forestry school. This initiative led to a second partnership with an employment center in neighboring New Richmond to
use the new distance-learning facility for retraining courses for people seeking employment. Increased awareness of the new technology
in the community is a particularly visible result of the project. As well,
students found summer jobs setting up the site, creating a Web page
and promoting the project locally. With the partnerships, the munic-

ipality expects to create more jobs in distance learning. As well, local businesses support the project and benefit from it.

Hill House Association, Pittsburgh, Pennsylvania (www.hillhouse. ckp.edu/hhcan/hhcan.html). In its role as a catalyst and convener for the Hill District of Pittsburgh, Pennsylvania, the Hill House Association has organized a network of public access sites to unify and serve the students, parents, residents, organizations, and businesses of the Hill District. The Hill House network provides electronic information and communication services addressing the needs of the broadest possible spectrum of Hill District residents while encouraging and providing assistance for the development of similar community access networks throughout the greater Pittsburgh area.

Current users of the Hill House center are able to use computers and the Internet during open lab hours. Members have access to an electronic mail box from which they can send and receive e-mail. Training in the basic use of computers, the Internet, and electronic mail is also provided. Each new member is assessed a $25 membership fee. Approximately half of the current members live in the Hill District with the remaining members from various Pittsburgh neighborhoods. One full-time staff person manages the lab, coordinates the volunteers, and develops the training program. The staff person constantly develops and recruits volunteers who serve as user assistants at public access sites. Currently there are twenty-five community access sites and information providers.

To develop the vision and prototype for the network, the Hill House Association has worked closely with Common Knowledge Pittsburgh, a component of the Pittsburgh Public Schools. Through this relationship working arrangements have been developed with Carnegie Mellon University and the University of Pittsburgh. Community networking is also being pursued at the Carnegie Library of Pittsburgh through the Three Rivers Free-Net. These developing relationships between Hill House and other organizations to build the community access network have been supported by Information Renaissance, the U.S. Commerce Department TIIAP program, and the City of Pittsburgh.

Lanark County, Ontario, Canada (www.lccin.on.ca). There are fifteen CAP sites in six communities throughout the county, just east of Ottawa, and together they make up the Lanark County Community Information Net (LCCIN). Sites up and running include Smiths Falls,

District Collegiate Institute, the Pakenham Public Library, and Perth's municipal offices. Nine more sites are on the way.

All this activity means new jobs in the county. A paid coordinator manages the sites. Students were employed to train many of the fifteen hundred people who signed up to learn about the Internet during its first year of operation. Local computer suppliers report sales growth of between 10 and 30 percent since the sites' launch. Computer packages that include modems have become increasingly popular as residents and businesspeople discover the benefits of the Internet. Users of the fifteen sites range from children to seniors, and community awareness of electronic communications is growing. When the CAP project began, Lanark County could boast no ISPs. Now, two or three can be found in each town in the county outside Ottawa's direct-dialing area (which means no long-distance charges for clients connecting to the Net!). The CAP project focuses on training and limits its Web-page design service to nonprofit community organizations—approximately 150 to date. The LCCIN Web site contains a database of eight hundred local organizations, which is kept current by the CAP student employees.

LapeerNet (www.lapeer.lib.mi.us). Based in rural Lapeer County, Michigan, this network operates under the aegis of the Greater Thumb Telecommunications Consortium (GTTC). The consortium is made up of six intermediate school districts, St. Clair County Community College, and the Mideastern Michigan Library Cooperative (MMLC) represented by Lapeer County Library. The coalition's mission is to support coordination of technology developments within the county. LapeerNet is a visible manifestation of this mission.

Lapeer County is a rural community fringed by metropolitan areas to the south and east. It is experiencing rapid growth and increased demands for information services. The county government is aware that advances in satellite, fiber optic, and digital telecommunications technologies make it possible for rural residents to hold information jobs with major employers and to enjoy a rural lifestyle enhanced by improved education, social services, and entertainment. Lapeer County recognizes that its economic and community development is dependent on the implementation of this enhanced telecommunications infrastructure. The public policy makers, businesses, and communication carriers see the potential in developing the physical and institutional infrastructure needed to make their rural area viable in this Information Age.

Lumby, British Columbia, Canada (www.monashee.com/). Started by a few keen volunteers, the Lumby CAP project has flourished and is now an important community resource. The site uses the well-equipped computer lab at J. W. Inglis Elementary School, where the school principal, Harry Adam, is one of the prime movers of the CAP initiative. The facility comprises thirty-three networked, Internet-ready Macintoshes, along with several scanners and an assortment of multimedia equipment. The project's steering committee built on this solid foundation by soliciting bids from service providers for e-mail and Internet connections. Through Okanagan Internet Junction, the winning firm, the committee plans to offer basic e-mail accounts to individuals for $10 and to families for $25. Volunteers refer those requiring more advanced connections to the firm, which returns a $25 commission to the site for each new customer. An enthusiastic cadre of volunteers provides Internet instruction for new and advanced users who can work on the site's computers outside school hours. To date, more than eight hundred people have received basic training. The site also acts as a catalyst for other developments. For example, the Monashee Web Programmers Alliance, an informal group of sixteen Internet enthusiasts, meets regularly to learn and practice Web-page production skills. Both the local chamber of commerce and the Monashee Tourism Information Service now have Web pages as a result of this group's efforts. Several local businesses—including a gourmet food producer, a breeder of American Black Coated Giant Schnauzers, and a company that sells a rare breed of horses—also have new Web pages and do a significant amount of their business through the Internet.

Miami and Carman, Manitoba, Canada (www.cici.mb.ca). Two communities in southern Manitoba have joined forces for their CAP project. Although Miami and Carman, Manitoba, each received CAP funding, they subsequently decided that they could accomplish more by working together. The neighboring towns, located southwest of Winnipeg, formed the Community Internet Cooperative Inc. (CICI), a not-for-profit cooperative that sustains itself primarily by selling Internet accounts and is run entirely by volunteers. Two committees administer the Miami and Carman sites: a technical committee purchases hardware and phone services and supervises the networking of the two communities' high schools, and a public relations committee promotes the initiative and associated training. Four students and a project coordinator operated the sites for the first summer. The team offered training programs, held open houses for seniors and farmers, researched preferred Internet sites for teachers, and interviewed local businesspeople about their information needs.

Now a number of local businesses make effective use of the Internet at the CAP sites. One local resident turned his hobby of crafting traditional longbows into a successful business by tapping into the world market the Internet provides. Teachers are integrating technology into the curriculum and using the Internet's vast information resources to prepare innovative history and current affairs lessons. Students' performance on class projects has improved because they can draw from the Internet's broad range of research material. They also find the Net useful for locating career information. The site has changed the life of one visually impaired man, opening up many new opportunities. He uses special technology at the facility that magnifies what's on the computer screen to read Internet versions of daily newspapers, check sports scores, read and write letters, and communicate with other visually impaired people.

CICI is now a thriving community effort. It features 140 customers and fourteen modems and holds its board meetings on interactive closed-circuit television. The public can visit the sites on Wednesday nights and take training by appointment. Organizers have earmarked any extra money they have to expand the initiative.

Montague, Prince Edward Island, Canada (www.peisland.com/cap/cappge.htm). The CAP team in Montague, Prince Edward Island, found an ambitious businessperson and technology enthusiast to run its site, and it has never looked back. The town has three community access sites with a total of five computers, thanks to the efforts of CAP site coordinator David Gregori. Gregori is a strong promoter of the business applications of the Internet as he also runs an Internet marketing and Web-page design company. Businesspeople and residents can sign on to the Internet at the public library, Montague Consolidated School, or Holland College's Montague Center. A substantial number of Montague residents have e-mail accounts through the workstations.

Northeastern Newfoundland, Canada (www.stemnet.nf.ca/CAP/central/Springdale). Organizers of the Indian River/Springdale CAP site know how to build on their strengths. They found that their isolated community is well placed to take advantage of the information technology revolution. For example, a major fiber-optic line passes near the town, giving it easy access to the Cable Atlantic network. The organizing team set out to convince the town's many businesses and community organizations that the Internet was an ideal way to do low-cost promotion and research. These efforts succeeded and local businesses have eagerly embraced new technology through a series of strategic partnerships with the CAP team. In the summer of 1996, three students set up "starter model" Web pages so individuals and organizations could easily put together Web sites on a trial basis. The students then suggested that the enthusiasts see what local Web-design businesses had to offer for more sophisticated pages. Organizations that develop Web pages can place them on the Springdale Cybermall free of charge. Barry Jackman, the CAP site coordinator, encourages the mall's "tenants" to focus on unique features that they and the town can offer. One Web page, for example, follows this advice by providing information on which salmon flies work best on the local river. Another page presents details on Newfoundland tartan craft.

Northern Francophones on the Net, Yukon, Canada

(francoculture.ca/afy/). Yukon's small, but active, francophone community has found a tool to help its members learn about the latest information technology and to come together as a group—its CAP site. Through its CAP project, the Association Franco-Yukonnaise shows northern francophones the value of the Internet as a resource and creates expertise in the related technology in the community. The association hopes to put together a training team and a group of volunteer resource people for local residents interested in the Internet. The association's office serves as the training facility. It features three computers equipped with French-language software and two dedicated lines so two people can be on the Net at once. This basic training dovetails nicely with courses offered locally, which means more business for private sector training firms.

To promote Internet use among local residents and businesspeople, the association offers a low-cost e-mail service. An e-mail address costs $4 a month. Online time goes for an additional $5 an hour. Several francophone businesspeople trained by CAP are now exploring the Internet as a venue for conducting business. One woman recently acquired equipment and an Internet account to establish an electronic presence for her company. Plans are in the works to develop an organization to maintain the site. The project owes most of its success to the active support of the association, which hopes to forge alliances with other organizations in the community, including a local French school that has just set up a well-equipped computer lab.

Paquetville, New Brunswick, Canada (www.crcp.nb.ca/cpnb). The organizers of the Paquetville, New Brunswick, CAP site made sure that the community's Web page would meet the information needs of local businesses. How? By asking questions. The organizing committee surveyed 450 companies, 90 percent of which are small businesses, from Paquetville and neighboring St. Isidore and Inkerman to find out what electronic information they require. An extensive database, which served as the foundation for the Paquetville Web site, contains the responses. The site itself features links to more than three thousand sources of business information, to institutions offering distance-learning programs in business, and to rural economic development sites. As Paquetville's billboard on the information highway, the Web site also showcases local products, services, and manufacturers. The groups behind the CAP site, including the municipal governments of the three communities, social groups, and a chamber of commerce, see the Internet as a key component of their business development plan. They want entrepreneurs to capitalize on the new technology. Training offered by CAP lets business owners develop technical knowledge and learn how to find information that will help them enlarge their client base. Soon, the general public will be invited to training sessions.

Several valuable alliances have resulted from the business consultations. The telephone company provided technical advice and six months of free Internet access. Another local business funds the Web site. The consultations also helped the organizing committee avoid duplicating services already offered by the private sector. Positive results are streaming in: business owners are keen to use the Net to market their companies, and local computer vendors, Internet providers, and Web-page designers all report increased sales.

Rankin Inlet, Northwest Territories, Canada (www.arctic.ca/ LUS/CAC.html). The Rankin Inlet community access center gives virtual visitors to the community's Web page a glimpse of a place many will never see in person. Bill Belsey, the CAP coordinator, explains, "Users can post stories on our Web page about Rankin to the rest of the world, which means they are no longer just on the receiving end of information. It increases confidence in our own way of life." The site is named Igalaaq, the Inuktitut word for "window," and is located at Leo Ussak Elementary School where Belsey teaches. In its first six months, Igalaaq had a thousand visitors, representing close to half the town's population. More than 450 people signed up for free e-mail accounts. Igalaaq attracts so much interest and curiosity because few people in Rankin Inlet, on the northwest coast of Hudson Bay, have home computers.

The community is experiencing exciting changes due to the Internet access the CAP site provides: the children's computer club for ages two to four meets once a week; grade three students correspond with pen pals from around the world; and a grade six class is learning Web-page design. Adults also use the site extensively, particularly the popular videoconferencing facility. The site comprises eighteen Apple computers equipped with English alphabet/Inuit syllabics keyboards, two scanners, and a Hewlett-Packard laser printer. The school library supplements the hardware with a collection of books and magazines about computers and the Internet. Experienced adult volunteers work assigned shifts with Maani Ulujuk High School senior students as cocustodians of Igalaaq.

The Rankin Inlet site, the first in the Northwest Territories, was initially funded by CAP and the territorial Department of Information Networks. Sakku Arctic Technologies, the local Internet service provider, sponsors the site's Web page, provides equipment, and underwrites Igalaaq's connection costs. Sakku, together with more than fifty other businesses, donated more than $108,000 in goods, services, and funds to the site in just one year. These Rankin Inlet contributors received the National Partners of Education Award from the Conference Board of Canada.

Rouyn-Noranda, Quebec, Canada (pyrite.uqat.uquebec.ca/~biblrn/). Library staff in northwestern Quebec are spreading the news about the Internet courtesy of the CAP project in Rouyn-Noranda. The Société des arts et des lettres de l'Abitibi-Témiscamingue, in cooperation with the Centre régional des services aux bibliothèques de l'Abitibi-Témiscamingue, will teach more than eight hundred members of library committees how to use computers and electronic information networks. "These people can then relay their knowledge to others in their communities," says the society's Normand Fink. "Seniors' groups and snowmobile clubs would likely be interested in the riches the Internet has to offer." "Libraries, long-time and stable presences in these communities, are ideal vehicles for this," adds Fink.

To make the information sharing happen, the society hopes to connect the seventy-five libraries in the communities of the Abitibi, Témiscamingue, and James Bay areas to the Inforoute biblio network. So far, the response has been overwhelming: twenty-five of the libraries have received CAP funding to create Web pages and to buy computers for public access and training. The CAP team is also encouraging the individual communities to create support organizations and to set up their own Web sites. The society has goals that extend far beyond the region as well. Negotiations are underway with other regional library service centers in Quebec, as well as in Ontario and Nova Scotia, to share resources. So far, though, training is the main focus of the project.

Southeastern Alberta, Canada (www.eidnet.org). Dave Hill, the coordinator of EIDnet, jokingly calls the network an "information canal for farmers." EID stands for Eastern Irrigation District, an organization that administers, operates, and maintains an extensive network of canals, reservoirs, and drains around the town of Brooks in southeastern Alberta. EIDnet's major objective is to offer Internet access to rural clients. Currently, it has 600 paying customers, and 250 area farmers and agricultural organizations have free accounts.

Local agricultural industries, a major growth engine for the area, are experiencing a revival courtesy of the enhanced information resources available through EIDnet. The district's Web page features information on agricultural research, biological research, marketing, precision farming, and meteorology, and contains links to a wide range of agricultural and related sites. Farmers can hook up to weather stations that track storms on radar and measure temperature and humidity. They can also easily retrieve important and relevant information on commodity prices and trends from the Net. E-mail lets users connect with government officials and agricultural researchers at convenient times and communicate with one another about a wide range of agricultural issues. Through their networking, farmers discovered that they can process much of their crop locally, allowing them to ship value-added products to their customers instead of raw materials.

A series of strategic partnerships underlies EID's ambitious program. These include agreements with Medicine Hat College to provide Internet training; with the Brooks Savings and Credit Union for financial support (in return credit union members get a discount on their EIDnet membership fee); with CNL Communications Networks Ltd. for technical support; and with Monarch Cable, which broadcasts fifteen-minute Internet training modules. EIDnet has had a strong impact on the community's economy. Four Web-page businesses and three new computer stores are up and running. CNL Communications Networks Ltd. brought in five times more business than it expected in its first year of operation as a result of its involvement with EIDnet, and now works for many corporate clients in Brooks.

Delivering Training, Support, and Technical Assistance

Delivering training, support, and technical assistance services is critical to ensuring that everyone in your community knows how to take advantage of all the great information services that you offer locally and that are available over the Internet. Providing these services is an important, distinguishing feature of most community networks since this is often the only source of free or low-cost assistance available to the public at large. Providing these services offers the community network an excellent opportunity to demonstrate its sustaining value to the community.

Among the service offerings you might consider:

Training classes—either instructor-led or self-paced classes.

Help desk—gives users an opportunity to have their particular questions or problems addressed. This service can be offered over the phone or online. The service can be staffed during particular hours and/or questions can be left on an answering machine and responded to later on.

Online assistance—providing online help enables the community network to provide assistance to users round the clock, every day of the year. Lists of "frequently asked questions," known as FAQs, can be created to meet the most typical user needs.

An innovative solution to delivering public access and training simultaneously has been worked out in Tallahassee, Florida. Software Solutions Now! (www.ssnow.com), a local computer training company, in partnership with the Leon County Public Library has opened its doors to the public at no charge on Tuesdays and Thursdays from 5:30 P.M. until 9 P.M. and on Saturdays from noon until 5:00 P.M. Solutions Now! staff are available to assist with any questions. Software may be loaded for personal use.

A large number of community networks describe online how they offer training and technical support services. In particular, the various

Missouri-based community networks have made these services a cornerstone of their offerings. I suggest you check the following sites for ideas to use in your own community:

Columbia Online Information Network (COIN) Virtual Help Desk   (www.coin.missouri.edu/about/coinhelp.html)

Lebanon-Laclede Information Online Network (LLION) Toolbox (www.llion.org/toolbox/index.html)

Ozarks Regional Information Online Network (ORION) (www.orion.org/help/index.html)

Westplex Information Network (WIN)   (www.win.org/)

Public Access Policies

Richard Nagler, head of adult services at the Farmington Community Library in Farmington Hills, Michigan, cautions that both obvious and hidden costs and problems come along with all the potential benefits of Internet access. Nagler offers the following suggestions to help you ensure that providing public access remains a positive experience for you and your users:

Make sure users understand that accessing the Internet from your facility is a privilege, not a right, and that there are certain responsibilities that go along with that privilege.

Clearly list those responsibilities.

Develop clearly articulated Internet usage policies and have them approved by your board. Make them visible and available to users. The Oswego Public Library in Oswego, Oregon, provides a list of public libraries' Internet policies on its Web site (www.ci.oswego.or.us/library/poli.htm), which you can review and adapt to your own particular situation.

Establish fair, clear, consistent rules and regulations that all staff members enforce.[2]

➤ Good Ideas

Listed below are thoughts and suggestions passed along by my interviewees that relate to public access:

➤ All staff have had to learn about the Internet and online communications. Some will really excel at it, which will motivate the rest of the staff and show them the value of all this.

➤ Citizens who learn about the community network through the library clearly associate the two; those who start on their own (or through some other organization) do not see the connection.

➤ Communicate to your library staff that it is OK for them to learn alongside the public. After all, this is a learning experience for everyone.

➤ Community networking gives librarians a chance—really for the first time ever—to truly serve the have nots. Get out on the circuit: work with the social workers today, with the local government people tomorrow, and so on.

➤ Don't be overly concerned about the "bad stuff" on the Internet. Problems don't arise nearly as often as one might imagine. Treat the viewing of offensive material as a behavior thing: it is against library policy to display offensive material. Since the public access workstations are out in the open, if patrons are found displaying offensive material they could be asked to leave.

➤ Don't give in to the hysteria that the Internet will make the library obsolete. Librarians have been sizing up technology and providing the community with information for a long time.

➤ Establish a broad volunteer base to help prevent burnout. Try to secure a two-year commitment from all volunteers.

➤ Even though your community may have many ISPs, consider yourself a safety net for access.

➤ It is important to view the community network as an educational vehicle: to make people aware of the potential of this technology and what it can do for them. This is a key piece and often doesn't get done.

- ➻ Let volunteers offer one-on-one training sessions, help organizations develop Web pages, perform hardware maintenance at public sites.

- ➻ Librarians have become the access providers. We guide, teach, and mentor the public: where to find it, how to find it, in what format, etc. Although more information is available now than ever before, more is also available in raw format. The public needs (and wants) someone who can analyze and interpret this raw content.

- ➻ Limit access to thirty minutes if people are waiting. Unfortunately, monitoring and enforcement are issues you may need to address.

- ➻ Locate all the technology coordinators throughout the community. Bring them together and show them how to access the resources that are available.

- ➻ Managing community network volunteers is not really different from managing other types of volunteers. Often you will find the community is overflowing with technical people interested in doing community service. You need to match the work that needs doing with the people willing to do the work.

- ➻ Of all the community networking roles the library can play, providing public access, training, and technical support are the most critical.

- ➻ Offer special orientation and training sessions for groups like the Rotary Club or the Medical Auxiliary.

- ➻ Originally our librarians perceived it as a problem that volunteers were helping people go online and use the Internet. But it has worked out fine.

- ➻ Public orientations to the Internet and the community network are still important.

- ➻ Resist your users' requests to have the community network become a full-service Internet provider (ISP). If you do so it will diminish your focus on developing community resources and capacity.

- ➻ Training the public to use the Internet can be a valuable lever to drive internal staff training.

- ➻ You may be surprised at the number of people who use the computers in the library who also have computers in their homes.

For More Information

Access to Computer Technology: Publications, Videos, Reports, Manuals, and More, by Carl Kucharski. (www.ctcnet.org/csk.html)

All-Out Internet Access, by Miles R. Fidelman. Chicago: American Library Association, 1997. ISBN: 0838906877.

Based on the experiences of the Cambridge, Massachusetts, library, Fidelman, who is president of the Center for Civic Networking, describes how to plan, implement, operate, and support Internet access. This book includes time-saving lists and worksheets.

American Library Association's Librarian's Guide to Cyberspace for Parents and Kids. (www.ala.org./parentspage/greatsites/)

Community Technology Activism: Giving Voice to Your Center, by Rainikka Corprew. (www.ctcnet.org/activ2.htm)

Community Technology Centers Review. (www.ctcnet.org/na6.html)

CTCNet and the Community Technology Center Movement, by Peter Miller. (www.ctcnet.org/peterm3.html)

Fortres Grand Corporation. (www.fortres.com/frmain.htm)

This company specializes in software products for public access workstations. Currently available products include: Fortres 101 (protects computer files, configurations, and programs from inexperienced or malicious users), Fortres Central Control (provides remote control of Fortres 101), Historian (tracks online usage and Web page access), and Cooler (disables features in a variety of software programs).

Gates Library Foundation. (www.glf.org/)

This Web site describes the activities of the foundation established by Microsoft's CEO, Bill Gates. The Gates Foundation is dedicated to partnering with public libraries to bring access to computers, the Internet, and digital information to patrons in low-income communities in the United States and Canada.

Hyper Technologies, Inc. (www.hypertec.com/)

This company specializes in software used to control public access computer workstations. Products include WINSelect Kiosk and

Ikiosk for disabling Windows program features, WINSelect Policy for disabling Windows desktop features, and WINSelect Tempo for controlling user access times.

ICONnect.   (www.ala.org/ICONN/toindex.html)

This Web site is sponsored by the American Association of School Librarians (AASL) and the American Library Association (ALA). Here, school library media specialists, teachers, and students will find the opportunity to learn the skills necessary to navigate the information superhighway. The site includes online courses, curriculum connections, minigrants, and an Internet Q&A service for K–12 students.

Internet Information Center (InterNIC) Tools for the Internet Trainer "15 Minute Series."   (rs.internic.net/nic-support/15min/)

Library and Community Technology Access Project. (www.ctcnet.org/libprop.html)

Missouri Express Resource Guides. (outreach.missouri.edu/moexpress/guides/)

Guide 12: Determining Internet Access Options, by Ted MacDonald

Guide 13: Providing Public Access, by Ted MacDonald, Dennis Minzes, and John Tharp

Guide 14: Providing Dial-Up Access, by Ted MacDonald

Guide 17: Providing Personal Services, by Ted MacDonald

Guide 18: Providing User Support Services, by Ted MacDonald

Guide 20: Education and Training, by Mary Simon Leuci

The Public-Access Computer Systems Review (PACS Review). (info.lib.uh.edu/pacsrev.html)

PACS Review is an electronic journal about end-user computer systems in libraries, published by the University of Houston Libraries. Although this journal is not published on a regular schedule, it is free and always includes interesting articles and hyperlinks to useful Internet resources. Topics include digital libraries, document delivery systems, electronic publishing, expert systems, hypermedia and multimedia systems, locally mounted databases, network-based information resources and tools, and online catalogs.

Resources on Technology Access and Community Technology Centers,
by Ana Yook.   (www.ctcnet.org/biblio.htm)

*The Role of Community Access Centers in Bridging the Technology
Gap,* by Susan Rose.   (www.ctcnet.org/rose/00title.htm)

Seattle Public Library Community Learning Labs.
(www.spl.lib.wa.us/learnlab/comlearn.html)

These labs provide free public access to multimedia computers
with Internet access, a variety of software, and computer training.

Technology Resource Institute (TRI).   (www.techresource.org/)

TRI works with public libraries to ensure that each community
will have access to the Internet and helps to train local library personnel in the use of these new tools. A key component of TRI projects is the fostering of a cooperative environment among the
various public-interest institutions to help create a sustainable
technology environment for the benefit of all citizens.

The Telementoring Revolution, by Felicia Robb.
(www.ctcnet.org/telement.html)

NOTES

1. Material in this section adapted from *Local Places, Global Connections: Libraries
   in the Digital Age,* Copyright 1997 Benton Foundation and Libraries for the
   Future. Used with permission. Copies are available from the Benton Foundation
   (www.benton.org), 1634 Eye Street, NW, Washington, DC 20006, phone:
   202/638-5770, or from Libraries for the Future (LFF) (www.lff.org), 121 W. 27th
   Street, Suite 1102, New York, NY 10001, phone: 212/352-2330, fax: 212/352-2342.

2. Adapted from "On My Mind: Home Front Horror Tales for Would-Be Public
   Internet Access Providers," *American Libraries* (May 1998): 40–41.

10

Evaluation and Sustainability

A comprehensive evaluation of the community networking activities is frequently overlooked. Unfortunately evaluation, like planning, is often treated as a luxury: something to be done when and if you have the resources. While it can be time-consuming and resource-intensive, it is vitally important that you document the impact of your efforts on the quality of life for the residents of your community.

The Importance of Evaluation

Evaluation enables you to document progress and, more importantly, to determine what impact your expenditure of resources (e.g., people's effort, time, and money) is having. That is, are you making a difference in your community? Remember that the overall goal of community networking is to ensure that local citizens have equal and affordable access to valuable electronic information; that more and more local information is available all the time; and that an ever greater range and number of local citizens are able to make effective use of electronic information and online services.

Therefore, your evaluation activities should be designed to answer questions such as:

What percentage of local residents uses the services provided by the community network?

To what extent do the demographics of community network users mirror the demographics of the community in general?

What benefits do current users derive from the community network? What service(s) could be improved?

What obstacles prevent nonusers from using the community network? How could these obstacles be overcome?

How does the community network affect use of and feeling about the traditional services provided by its coalition partners? For example, how does the community network affect library use?

What have the community networking activities done to improve the quality of life for local residents and the economic development of the region served?

Keep in mind that the community network—as with any computer technology application—is but a means to an end. Your real goal is to improve your community. Evaluating your efforts helps ensure that you improve the community in tangible, measurable ways and that the community is better off as a result of your efforts.

Since virtually all community networks seem to exist on less-than-sufficient resources, day-to-day activities always seem to take precedence over evaluation. Therefore, it may be helpful to construct evaluation activities that become a part of the ongoing activities or ones that can be carried out by persons outside the daily maelstrom.

It is important to distinguish between use and impact, even though each is important when it comes to evaluating your community networking initiatives. Use documents activity; impact measures results. Like door counts in the library, use data are frequency tabulations of the number of accesses to the particular services that the community network provides. Most helpful use data should be easy to collect. For instance, server-based operating systems very often include a log feature that can automatically keep track of activities occurring on the server. Many can be set to cycle themselves automatically. Most e-mail and Web server programs come with similar logging features. Auxiliary programs can provide a wealth of data about who is using your system and what information appears to be most popular.

Help desk staff or volunteers can be instructed to keep a log of the number of people they assist, whom they assist (e.g., new users, experienced users, information providers), how this assistance was provided (e.g., in person, by phone, online), and the type of assistance they provided.

Public access terminals can track automatically their number of log-ins. Site monitors can keep door counts and record time periods.

Have sign-in sheets at training sessions and ask participants to provide basic demographic data about themselves and their computer and online capabilities. Let them know why you are collecting these data. Assure them that the data are for research and evaluation purposes only and will be kept strictly confidential.

On the other hand, impact evaluation measures results: the measurable effect of the community networking activities on the community. Evaluations of this sort are behavioral and qualitative and, hence, cannot be measured with numeric counts alone.

I have listed some suggestions below that you can use to minimize the strain on your existing resources and get the most out of your evaluation efforts.

Recruit faculty from the local college or university to assist with evaluation activities. Don't restrict your recruitment efforts to faculty whose work is directly related to community networking. Faculty in almost every discipline are trained researchers who can advise you on every aspect of evaluation and can implement research projects using a variety of methodologies.

Consider multiple methods for collecting data about your various projects and from your various stakeholders. Possible data collection methods include interviews, focus groups, observation, and surveys. There are pros and cons to each method. While it is beyond the scope of this book to discuss these methods in any detail, consult your faculty advisor to determine the best method to employ.

Review evaluations done for traditional human services programs as models for evaluating your community networking initiatives. Suitable examples may be readily available from your local government or nonprofit agency partners or through the library.

Evaluating the Collaboration

Margret Dugan suggests that the evaluation process should not only determine how well the project meets its goals and outcomes but should analyze process-related issues too. She suggests making sure the evaluation enables you to understand fully and objectively such issues as (1) the sequence of events from program planning through implementation; (2) the program's structure: its components and delivery methods; (3) the context in which the program takes place; (4) the unanticipated results; and (5) the degree of community awareness.[1]

Steven Mayer suggests evaluation activities, like the programs themselves, should be designed to build capacity within the community. "This position suggests that communities are strengthened when they can build upon their strengths and assets rather than be made to focus on their needs or deficits. Evaluation, too, can be constructed from this perspective."[2] Mayer suggests that since the people who could benefit most from the evaluation are not other external evaluators or social scientists, it is unnecessary to design evaluations that conform to their expectations. Rather, it is far more beneficial to design evaluations that will be read or heard by those involved in the project being evaluated, by "similar" persons elsewhere in the community (both physical and virtual), and by those who work with or directly support the project. These are the people who can act upon the findings and recommendations.

Michael Winer and Karen Ray, in *Collaboration Handbook: Creating, Sustaining, and Enjoying the Journey,* describe how it is important first to value evaluation, then to set up measures and methods.* While evaluation ideally begins at the first meeting, most collaborations do not formalize assessment until they are ready to act. Yet we need to continually measure performance against expectations in both processes—how the group functions, and results—what the group achieves.

If the collaboration has observed its milestones, it will have the data it needs to proceed. If not, go back and review the previous steps and ensure that all the necessary documentation has been completed and gathered. Next, ask a subgroup to lay out the data according to the

* From *Collaboration Handbook: Creating, Sustaining, and Enjoying the Journey,* by Michael Winer and Karen Ray, copyright 1994 Amherst H. Wilder Foundation. Used with permission. For more information on Wilder Foundation Publications, call 1-800-274-6024.

Process Evaluation	*Results Evaluation*
1. State the separate self-interests of each organization and how it will know its self-interests are being met.	1. State the desired community benefits and how the collaboration will know if the effort is successful.
2. Note when milestones are accomplished and what helped and hindered their accomplishment.	2. Outline the methods being used.
3. Describe communication processes between members of the collaboration.	3. Summarize critical junctures.
4. Summarize the collaboration's impact on its member organizations. How has each contributed? How did the collaboration change the way each organization does business?	4. Describe how the characteristics of the community being targeted (geographic, ethnic population, sector, field, service recipient) have changed, the number and diversity of the people involved, their reaction to the collaboration and its methods, and changes in the community that might be attributed to the effort.
5. Note side effects. Who else became involved because of the collaboration? How does their effort help the community network?	5. Note side effects.

various process and results categories. At this time, the subgroup creates other categories as needed, then assigns responsibilities for seeking other data (if needed), analyzing information, and summarizing results. If all this seems formidable, contact someone who specializes in evaluation.

Finally, the whole group reviews the plan. Then ask key decision makers in the collaborating organizations and other important stakeholders if the plan will provide the information they need to continue supporting the collaborative effort. After making any needed changes, ratify the evaluation plan.

Collaborations must constantly seek feedback by listening everywhere, and continually assess their efforts in accord with their developmental stage. The purpose is continuous improvement. Thus, evaluation becomes integral to the joint effort. What questions do we ask on an ongoing basis?

Is the effort effective? Are we achieving our objectives by benefiting the community and meeting our own self-interests?

Is the effort adequate? Are we using enough resources to achieve results?

Is the effort efficient? Have we expended minimum time, money, and energy to build maximum relationships and take complete action?

What lessons have we learned? What do we now know about the relationships we have built and need to build, and the work we have done and need to do?

Honest answers to these questions create opportunities for further change, refinements, and improved results. Communicating those results builds increased support from member organizations and from those who might be persuaded to join the effort.

Keep in mind that the sole purpose of collaboration is for organizations to achieve results they are more likely to achieve together than alone. Sometimes the purpose of the group becomes fixed, and it disregards evaluative data that demand a change in practice. To achieve both our self-interests and community benefits, we must accept the validity of evaluation information, especially when it says we—individually and organizationally—need to change. The evaluation process may point out the need for the group to reemphasize adaptability and flexibility, retire some members, or add new members.

Changing staff and membership patterns, resources and linkages with other organizations, and formal structures within the coalition may affect the outcomes and impact of a coalition. The costs and benefits of an extensive needs assessment and planning process should also be considered. If needs assessment and planning are time- and resource-consuming and do not result in better outcomes, coalitions may decide to put their efforts elsewhere.[3]

In any event, spread the lessons you have learned from your collaboration. Evaluation findings that stay on the shelf unread and unheeded are worthless, no matter how legitimate the process for discovery. All media should be considered for disseminating worthwhile findings—print, broadcast, workshops, storytelling, and electronic bulletin boards.[4]

Mayer further suggests that you use the evaluation process to create linkages among and between the various individuals and groups who participate in and have an effect on your programs. "Recom-mendations should be written that allow community organizations to mobilize and strengthen the commitment they bring to their work, increase the financial and other resources usable for strengthening their work, and further develop the skills needed to make their work effective."[5]

For More Information

An Analysis of Boulder Community Network Usage, by Sam Harsh. (bcn.boulder.co.us/community/resources/harsh/article2.html)

A Critical Study of Three Free-Net Community Networks, by Ben Stallings.   (ofcn.org/whois/ben/Free-Nets/)

A Diverse Group Has Access to the Boulder Community Network, by Sam Harsh.   (bcn.boulder.co.us/community/resources/harsh/article1.html)

Bibliography: Online Resources about Community Network Evaluations, by Kim Gregson, doctoral student in information science, Indiana University. (php.indiana.edu/~kgregson/main_menu.html)

Blacksburg Electronic Village Design History Project. (history.bev.net/bevhist/)

This project, funded by the National Science Foundation, is documenting the development and implementation of the BEV using an online database.

The Boulder Community Network: Access and Use.   (bcn.boulder.co.us/community/resources/harsh/harshproject.html)

Building Community in Rural America: A Replicable Model for Community Networks, by Andrew Cohill and Andrea Kavanaugh. (www.bev.net/project/research/NTIA-95.html)

Communities On-Line: Community Based Computer Networks, by Anne Beamish.   (alberti.mit.edu/arch/4.207/anneb/thesis/toc.html)

Chapter 3 of this master's thesis includes information about the role of monitoring, reasons for failure, how assessment has been done, short-term goals (sustainability, growth), long-term goals (access, democratic participation, community development), who benefits from evaluation, and a bibliography.

Community Technology Centers: Impact on Individual Participants and Their Communities, by June Mark, Janet Cornebise, and Ellen Wahl.   (www.ctcnet.org/eval.html)

Evaluating the Impact of Networking on K–12 Education Reform, by John Burton and Andrea Kavanaugh.
(www.bev.net/project/research/NSF96.html)

Evaluation of Internet Training Classes.   (www.bev.net/education/ntia/evaluation/Auburn_evaluation_results.html)

Frequency of Use for Regularly Used Features on the National Capital FreeNet, by Andrew Patrick, Alex Black, and Thomas Whalen. (debra.dgbt.doc.ca/services-research/features/features.html)

Implications of Access Methods and Frequency of Use for the National Capital FreeNet, by Andrew S. Patrick and Alex Black.
(debra.dgbt.doc.ca/services-research/survey/connections/)

Internet Access and Use: Boulder Community Network Users, by Mary Virnoche.   (sobek.colorado.edu/~virnoche/results2.html)

Internet Training Class: Evaluation Form.   (www.bev.net/education/ntia/evaluation/Auburn_evaluation_form.html)

Missouri Express Resource Guides.
(outreach.missouri.edu/moexpress/guides/)

> *Guide 24: Keys to Sustaining a CIN through Evaluation,* by Mary Simon Leuci

> *Guide 25: Sustaining the Community Network through Evaluation,* by Kenneth Pigg

Personal and Social Impacts of Going On-Line: Lessons from the National Capital FreeNet, by Andrew Patrick.
(debra.dgbt.doc.ca/services-research/survey/impacts/)

Quarterly Performance Reports: Blacksburg Electronic Village.
(www.bev.net/project/research/)

Report on Phase One Activities: User Assessment. Linking Distributed Regional Resources—A Model for Regional Information Systems. (www.solinet.net/monticello/pip/ntia95.htm)

Rich, Young, Male, Dissatisfied Computer Geeks? Demographics and Satisfaction from the National Capital FreeNet, by Andrew S. Patrick, Alex Black, and Thomas E. Whalen. (debra.dgbt.doc. ca/services-research/survey/demographics/vic.html)

Services on the Information Highway: Subjective Measures of Use and Importance from the National Capital FreeNet, by Andrew Patrick. (debra.dgbt.doc.ca/services-research/survey/services/)

Use and Impact of Community Networking in the Blacksburg Electronic Village, by Andrea Kavanaugh and Scott Patterson. (www.bev.net/project/research/Research.Highs.1_97.html)

NOTES

1. "Participatory and Empowerment Evaluation: Lessons Learned in Training and Technical Assistance," by Margret A. Dugan. In *Empowerment Evaluation: Knowledge and Tools for Self-Assessment and Accountability,* edited by David M. Fetterman, Shakeh J. Kaftarian, and Abraham Wandersman (Thousand Oaks, Calif.: Sage Publications, 1996).
2. "Building Community Capacity with Evaluation Activities That Empower," by Steven E. Mayer. In *Empowerment Evaluation: Knowledge and Tools for Self-Assessment and Accountability,* edited by David M. Fetterman, Shakeh J. Kaftarian, and Abraham Wandersman (Thousand Oaks, Calif.: Sage Publications, 1996), 334.
3. "The Plan Quality Index: An Empowerment Evaluation Tool for Measuring and Improving the Quality of Plans," by Frances D. Butterfoss, Robert M. Goodman, Abraham Wandersman, Robert F. Valois, and Matthew J. Chinman. In *Empowerment Evaluation: Knowledge and Tools for Self-Assessment and Accountability,* edited by David M. Fetterman, Shakeh J. Kaftarian, and Abraham Wandersman (Thousand Oaks, Calif.: Sage Publications, 1996).
4. Mayer, op. cit., p. 337.
5. Ibid.

APPENDIX

Learning from Others

This appendix contains information about a variety of online resources of interest to you as you plan, develop, and implement community networking projects. This information was adapted from the included organizations' Web sites. Hyperlinks to these and other pertinent sites are available from my Web site (www.libsci.sc.edu/stephen/bajjaly.htm).

Access for All (www.accessforall.org) is a New York coalition of organizations formed to share information and resources concerning telecommunications legislation and public policy.

Access Point (www.accesspt.com/) applies online technology to help individuals and organizations make a difference. Includes the Nonprofit Professionals Network, which offers online links to information on fund-raising, tax and legal issues, technology, marketing, and PR.

Action without Borders (www.idealist.org) is a global network of individuals and organizations sharing ideas, information, and resources to help build a world where all people can live free, dignified, and productive lives. Action without Borders works through the Internet and through local chapters to promote and facilitate collaboration, volunteerism, and investment in support of these goals.

Alliance for Community Media (www.alliancecm.org/) is committed to ensuring everyone's access to electronic media. The Alliance accomplishes this goal through public education, advancing a positive legislative and regulatory environment, building coalitions, and supporting local organizing efforts. A nonprofit, national membership organization founded in 1976, the Alliance represents the interests of over 1,000 public, educational, and governmental ("PEG") access organizations (generally known as "public access") and public access Internet centers throughout the country. It also represents the interests of an estimated 1.5 million individuals, through their local religious, community, charitable, and other groups, who utilize PEG access television centers and Internet providers to speak to their memberships and their larger communities.

Alliance for Public Technology (www.apt.org/) is a nonprofit membership organization based in Washington, D.C. Membership is open to those concerned with fostering access to affordable and useful information and communication services and technologies by all people.

American Library Association (ALA) (www.ala.org) is the oldest and largest library association in the world, and its fifty-seven thousand members represent all types of libraries—public, school, academic, state, and special. ALA offers an extensive array of programs, educational opportunities, conferences, and publications for librarians and the general public interested in library issues.

AmeriCorps (www.cns.gov/americorps/index.html) is the national service program that allows people of all ages and backgrounds to earn help paying for education in exchange for a year of service. AmeriCorps members meet community needs by providing a wide range of community services. Programs under the AmeriCorps umbrella include: AmeriCorps*VISTA, State and National Direct, and the National Civilian Community Corps.

Argus Clearinghouse (www.clearinghouse.net/) provides a central access point for Internet resource topic guides. Guides are available for the following topic areas: arts and humanities; business and employment; communication; computers and information technology; education; engineering; environment; government and law; health and medicine; places and people; recreation; science and math; social sciences and social issues.

ArtsWire (www.artswire.org) provides online communications services to artists and community-based cultural groups.

Aspen Institute (www.aspeninst.org) in Aspen, Colorado, is an international nonprofit educational institution dedicated to enhancing the quality of leadership through informed dialogue. It convenes men and women who represent diverse viewpoints and backgrounds from business, labor, government, the professions, the arts, and the nonprofit sector to relate timeless ideas and values to the foremost challenges facing societies, organizations, and individuals. A wide variety of publications is available.

The Institute for Information Studies, a joint project of the Aspen Institute and Nortel, each year commissions a collection of papers focusing on a particular topic relating to the impact of communications and information technology, from a variety of perspectives, which together are published as an Annual Review.

The Internet as Paradigm, 1997 Annual Review. This volume explores the Internet phenomenon, its promise and possibilities, from seven different perspectives, with papers by Anthony M. Rutkowski on organization and technology, Hal R. Varian on economics, Brian Kahin on business, Bruce W. McConnell on governance, Michael Cornfield and F. Christopher Arterton on politics, Beverly Hunter on education, and James F. Moore on complex adaptive systems, and an introduction by John Hindle. 1997. ISBN: 0898432049.

The Emerging World of Wireless Communications, 1996 Annual Review. This volume examines the role wireless technology will play as part of the nation's future information infrastructure from six different perspectives, with papers by Michael L. Katz on policy and regulation, Lewis J. Paper on politics, Dale N. Hatfield on digital technology, James E. Katz on adapting to technological change, Maryam Alavi on business applications, and Stuart N. Brotman on the international dimension, and an introduction by Fred W. (Rick) Weingarten. 1996. ISBN: 0898431859.

Crossroads on the Information Highway: Convergence and Diversity in Communications Technology, 1995 Annual Review. This volume examines the convergence of information technologies from six different perspectives, with papers by Robert Crandall on economics, John Midwinter on technology, James F. Moore on business, Eric Vogt on international implications and the structure of work, Jorge Reina Schement on individual stakes, and Barbara Kurshan and Cecilia Lenk on education, and an introduction by Richard P. Adler. 1995. ISBN: 0898431646.

The Knowledge Economy: The Nature of Information in the Twenty-First Century, 1993–94 Annual Review. This volume provides a window into the thought of tomorrow on the nature of information from six different perspectives, with papers by Stephen H. Haeckel and Richard L. Nolan on technology, Roger G. Noll on economics, Blake Ives and Sirkka L. Jarvenpaa on business, Peter F. Cowhey and M. Margaret McKeown on world affairs,

Sara B. Kiesler and Pamela Hinds on sociology, and Charles R. McClure on education, and an introduction by Nicholas Johnson. 1994. ISBN: 0898431476.

The Forum on Communications and Society (FOCAS) convenes CEO leaders of the business, government, and nonprofit sectors on an annual basis to define an important issue for the national agenda, identify the barriers to progress, and seek innovative ways that new communications and information technologies and other resources can be used to expand opportunity for all Americans.

Creating a Learning Society: Initiatives for Education and Technology, by Amy K. Garmer and Charles M. Firestone, is the first report of the Aspen Institute Forum on Communications and Society, a group of twenty-five CEOs from business, government, and the nonprofit sector. This report on education and technology addresses specific issues in the K–12 classroom, as well as broader issues of lifelong learning outside the classroom. The report offers a range of initiatives for overcoming barriers to funding technology in schools and training teachers how to integrate technology into the classroom. 1996. ISBN: 0898431972.

The Aspen Conference on Telecommunications Policy annually convenes key decision makers from business; federal, state, and local governments; academia; and the nonprofit sector to address issues of telecommunications regulation, development, and public policy.

Implementing Universal Service after the 1996 Telecommunications Act, Robert M. Entman, rapporteur. Report of the Eleventh Annual Aspen Conference on Telecommunications Policy. This report summarizes the Conference's suggestions for universal service policy options, generally, and financing options for schools and libraries, specifically, which were submitted to the Federal-State Joint Board on Universal Service in September 1996. The report includes an appendix with sections of the Telecommunications Act of 1996 that relate to universal service. 1996. ISBN: 0898431905.

The Communications Devolution: Federal, State, and Local Relations in Telecommunications Competition and Regulation, Robert Entman, rapporteur. In the context of landmark communications legislation, *The Communications Devolution* examines the forces shaping the competitive world of telecommunications, and offers federal, state, and local regulators a road map to resolving jurisdictional disputes and promoting effective competition. 1996. ISBN: 0898431905.

The annual Roundtable on Information Technology examines the global implications of advanced communications systems and other digital services for commerce, nation-states, societies, communities, and the individual.

The Networked Society: How New Technologies Are Transforming Markets, Organizations, and Social Relationships, David Bollier, rapporteur. Report of the Fifth Annual Aspen Institute Roundtable on Information Technology. This report explores how electronic networking—the Internet and intranets—is transforming commerce, organizational performance and leadership, business and social relationships, and personal identity and allegiances. 1997.

The Future of Electronic Commerce, David Bollier, rapporteur. Examines the communications and information technologies that are redefining the fundamental conditions and relationships of commercial transactions, and the implications of the new electronic commerce for individuals, businesses, and society. 1996. ISBN: 0898431883.

The Future of Community and Personal Identity in the Coming Electronic Culture, David Bollier, rapporteur. This report concentrates on issues of personal identity, community building, and setting boundaries in our lives and our environment, and includes a background paper by Charles M. Firestone entitled, "The New Intermediaries." 1995. ISBN: 0898431662.

The Promise and Perils of Emerging Information Technologies, David Bollier, rapporteur. This report of the Second Annual Aspen Roundtable on Information Technology, held in 1993, explores the use of complex adaptive systems as a model for determining information technology's role in both the workplace and diverse societal settings. It includes a background paper by John Seely Brown, Paul Duguid, and Susan Haviland entitled, "Towards Informed Participants: Six Scenarios in Search of Democracy in the Electronic Age," that offers progressive scenarios of how the interaction of humans and information technologies might influence and affect democratic life in the coming decade. 1993. ISBN: 0898431492.

The Information Evolution: How New Information Technologies Are Spurring Complex Patterns of Change, David Bollier, rapporteur. This is the report of the first annual Aspen Roundtable on Information Technology, held in 1992, which examined the impact of information technologies on democratic institutions and values. The conference report explores the use of a new paradigm, that of coevolving complex adaptive systems, for thinking about information, information technologies, and information-oriented societies. 1993. ISBN: 0898431328.

The Markle Series: Enhancing the Social Benefits of New Electronic Technologies is an occasional series funded by the John and Mary R. Markle Foundation. Each report in this series addresses a specific area in which new electronic technologies can benefit individuals and society.

Elections in Cyberspace: Toward a New Era in American Politics, Anthony Corrado and Charles M. Firestone, editors. The proliferation of candidate Web pages and other politically oriented Internet sites during the 1996 campaign foreshadows the potential impact that new communications and information technologies will have on the American political process in the future. Will they enhance the democratic spirit of America or further exacerbate the sense of alienation within the electorate? This report describes the new political uses of technology and addresses the adequacy of current election laws and regulations in coping with campaigns and elections in cyberspace. The report includes an appendix with four commissioned papers—one essay and three scenarios—describing campaigns and elections in the future. 1996. ISBN: 0898432022.

Toward an Information Bill of Rights and Responsibilities, Charles M. Firestone and Jorge Reina Schement, editors. This volume offers three sets of first principles for understanding the rights and responsibilities of individuals and governments in an information society. These include first principles for (1) communications rights and responsibilities, (2) privacy, and (3) information as property in the emerging digital society. 1995. ISBN: 0898431727.

Democratic Designs for Electronic Town Meetings, by Jeffrey B. Abramson. This paper looks at the goals that have historically been set for democratic town meetings, and then considers how these goals may be met through the use of modern communications and information technologies. Among other issues, the paper considers the problems of setting a neutral and fair agenda, giving the audience a stake in the outcome, and ensuring equitable electronic access to the meeting. 1993. ISBN: 0898431409.

SeniorNet Services: Towards a New Electronic Environment for Seniors, Gary Arlen, rapporteur. This 1991 conference report examines the development of SeniorNet, a nonprofit computer training program for seniors that has grown into a full-fledged community of maturing adults. The report explores the social benefits of computer networking as well. This is Forum Report 15 in the series, The Aspen Institute Project on Enhancing the Social Benefits of New Electronic Technologies. 1991. ISBN: 0898431107.

Electronic Media Regulation and the First Amendment: A Perspective for the Future, David Bollier, rapporteur. This report offers an examination of the three major legal paradigms that have traditionally governed communications media, and how the "purity" of these models is challenged by the new electronic media. It discusses the scarcity of broadcasting frequencies, the Fairness Doctrine, cable regulation, and common carrier regulation. The report then goes on to propose ten new theories of the First Amendment in the era of electronic media. This is Forum Report 14 in the series, The Aspen Institute Project on Enhancing the Social Benefits of New Electronic Technologies. 1991. ISBN: 0898431034.

Benton Foundation (www.benton.org), through its Communications Policy Project, promotes public interest values and noncommercial services for the National Information Infrastructure through research, policy analysis, print, video and online publishing, and outreach to nonprofits and foundations. Its Web site contains updates on communications policy and upcoming events; a forum for discussion; publications such as bulletins, policy briefings, and working papers; and links to hundreds of online communications and public interest resources.

Catalog of Federal Domestic Assistance (FDAC) (www.gsa.gov/fdac/) is a searchable, governmentwide database of federal programs, projects, services, and activities that provide assistance or benefits to the American public. The site includes information about financial and nonfinancial assistance programs administered by departments and establishments of the federal government.

CAUSE (cause-www.colorado.edu) was established to support the transformational changes occurring in higher education through the effective management and use of information resources—technology, services, and information.

Center for Technology in the Public Library (www.spl.org/cfthome/cfthome.htm) is one of three centers that can shape the future of the Seattle Public Library. The Center is intended to function as a catalyst and linking agent, bringing together the needs of the public, the skills of information professionals, and the products of high technology companies. Research and development efforts emphasize projects that are of special interest to Seattle, but can also be replicated in other libraries.

Center for the Study of Online Community (netscan.sscnet.ucla.edu/csoc/), based at UCLA, seeks to present and foster studies that focus on how computers and networks alter people's capacity to form groups, organizations, and institutions and how those social formations are able to serve the collective interests of their members.

CivicSource (civicsource.org/) has been established by the Academy of Leadership at the University of Maryland to link individuals, businesses, communities, and movements with the resources to meet the needs of a new century of civic activism and transforming leadership. Through CivicSource and its link to the nation's most prominent leadership scholars, the Academy of Leadership is developing a national database of leadership development programs and resources, and providing information to support citizen action on public issues.

Civic Practices Network (CPN) (www.cpn.org/index.html) is a collaborative, nonpartisan project dedicated to bringing practical tools for public problem solving into community and institutional settings across America. The common mission of CPN members and affiliates is to tell stories of civic innovation, share practical wisdom, and exchange the most effective tools available. CPN documents case studies, training manuals, "best practice" guides, and evaluative tools so that all of us can become more skillful about the public work that we do. CPN maps innovative projects around the country, and helps participating organizations locate other civic assets and partners.

Coalition for Healthier Cities and Communities (healthycommunities.org/) is a partnership of public, private, and nonprofit sector organizations collaborating to focus attention and resources on improving the health and quality of life of communities through community-based development.

Common Knowledge: Pittsburgh (CK:P) (info.ckp.edu/) is a research project working to develop a scalable networking infrastructure in support of curricular activities and educational reform. The original CK:P collaboration involved the Pittsburgh Public Schools, the Pittsburgh Supercomputing Center, and the University of Pittsburgh.

Communications Catalyst (www.rtk.net/comcat/) is designed to help the nonprofit community use the full resources of the "information superhighway" by tracking federal government and other information about communications grants and policy; distributing this information widely; and providing technical assistance to nonprofits in developing, managing, and evaluating model projects involving the information superhighway. This project pulls together online resources to help community-oriented nonprofit organizations better find and apply for federal grants. Includes links to online information resources for federal grant seekers and NII-related federal grants. Also includes a list of conferences, training sessions, and regular meetings that may be of interest to nonprofits that wish to learn more about the information superhighway (its role and potential for the nonprofit community), telecommunications and NII policy, and pursuing federal government grants. Communications Catalyst, 1742 Connecticut Avenue, NW, Washington, DC 20009. Phone: 202/234-8494; fax: 202/234-8584; e-mail: comcat@comcat.org.

Communities Online (www.communities.org.uk) is a three-year British initiative to develop and support online networking in ways that will enhance and sustain local communities. Main activities of this campaign (which runs through 2000) include operating a Web site and discussion areas that promote community networking. With start-up funding from the British government's Department of Trade and Industry and other partners and sponsors, the Communities

Online campaign is designed to support small local initiatives and to promote larger public-private community partnerships using digital technologies.

CompuMentor (www.compumentor.org/) is a nonprofit technical assistance group that helps volunteers, schools, and nonprofits work together to solve computer problems. This site contains information about the services offered to volunteers, nonprofits, and schools.

Computer Professionals for Social Responsibility (CPSR) (www.cpsr.org/) is a public interest alliance of computer scientists and others concerned about the impact of computer technology on society.

Crossroads (crossroads.dialog.com/), sponsored by Dialog Corporation, aims to be a community of interest for the information professional.

Education Development Center (EDC) (www.edc.org/home.html), a nonprofit research and development organization, creates and administers innovative projects around the world. These projects span many fields, joining research with practice to address important challenges in health, education, human rights, technology, and the environment. Despite their diversity, all of EDC's projects are united by the conviction that education is crucial to human development and that learners are active, problem-solving participants in the process.

Electronic Frontier Foundation (www.eff.org/) is a nonprofit civil liberties organization working in the public interest to protect privacy, free expression, and access to public resources and information online, as well as to promote responsibility in new media.

Electronic Policies Network (EPN) (epn.org/) is an online project of *The American Prospect* Magazine. The aim of EPN is to contribute to a renewal of America's democratic traditions by presenting a practical and convincing vision of liberal philosophy, politics, and public life. The "Idea Central" section of its Web site includes hyperlinks related to civic participation and politics including new technology, government, and civic life.

Federal Information Exchange (FEDIX) (web.fie.com) is a free online information retrieval service of federal opportunities for the education and research communities. Key federal agencies support FEDIX under a cooperative agreement from the Department of

Energy, Office of Science Education and Technical Information. Participating agencies use FEDIX as an outreach tool to promote enhanced communication to colleges, universities, and other educational and research organizations. FEDIX is a user-friendly, one-stop source of current federal funding information that benefits educators and researchers.

Global Information Infrastructure Commission (www.gii.org) has been created to foster private sector leadership and private-public sector cooperation in the development of information networks and services to advance global economic growth, education, and quality of life. The GIIC is an independent, nongovernmental initiative involving leaders from developing as well as industrialized countries.

Global Knowledge Partnership (www.globalknowledge.org/) is the home of a growing partnership and dialogue focused on harnessing knowledge and information as tools of sustainable and equitable development and mobilizing the innovations and resources of the information revolution as tools to empower the world's poor.

HandsNet (www.igc.apc.org/handsnet/) is a national nonprofit organization that promotes information sharing, cross-sector collaboration, and advocacy among individuals and organizations working on a broad range of public-interest issues.

iComm (www.icomm.ca) is a nonprofit, Internet-based organization that exists to help other nonprofit, charitable, and community organizations by giving them Internet services and volunteer support. Think of it as a community network helping groups instead of individuals.

I*EARN (www.igc.apc.org/iearn/) enables young people to undertake projects designed to make a meaningful contribution to the health and welfare of the planet and its people.

Information Access Institute (IAI) (information.org/) is a nonprofit organization designed to help libraries, museums, archives, and other information service organizations plan and implement Internet servers. IAI specializes in providing public access to searchable information collections in compliance with national and international standards. Those collections can include catalogs or databases, digital images, exhibits combining text with images, scanned documents, digital sound files, and digital video.

Institute for Global Communications (www.igc.org/igc/) aims to expand and inspire movements for peace, economic and social justice, human rights, and environmental sustainability around the world by providing and developing accessible computer networking tools.

International Govnews Project (www.govnews.org/) seeks to stimulate electronic access to public government information and electronic "open democracy" by establishing the framework for a dedicated government hierarchy on the Internet's UseNet news service where needed public information can be easily made available and discussed.

The Internet Society (www.isoc.org/) is a nongovernmental international organization for global cooperation and coordination for the Internet and its internetworking technologies and applications. The society's individual and organizational members are bound by a common stake in maintaining the viability and global scaling of the Internet. They comprise the companies, government agencies, and foundations that have created the Internet and its technologies as well as innovative new entrepreneurial organizations contributing to maintain that dynamic.

John T. and Catherine D. MacArthur Foundation (www.macfdn. org) home page provides information about the Foundation's programs, how to apply, recent grants, links to philanthropy resources, and other materials. The Foundation is dedicated to helping groups and individuals foster lasting improvement in the human condition. The Foundation seeks the development of healthy individuals and effective communities, peace within and among nations, responsible choices about human reproduction, and a global ecosystem capable of supporting healthy human societies. The Foundation pursues this mission by supporting research, policy development, dissemination, education and training, and practice. The Program on Human and Community Development supports work in community development, the arts, economic opportunity, youth development, education, mental health, research, and other areas.

Libraries for the Future (LFF) (www.lff.org) is a national nonprofit organization of public library advocates. LFF educates and activates current and potential library users to become advocates and works to enhance the relationship between libraries and communities—particularly those with limited resources. The LFF program promotes community participation and universal access to literacy, lifelong learning, and information—essential tools for democracy.

LibraryNet (www.ualberta.ca/~cthrashe/webcrew/libnet/) is a cooperative venture on the part of Canadian libraries, librarians, and the federal government to facilitate connectivity and use of the information highway in Canada. LibraryNet offers a wealth of information resources for librarians. This site contains relevant, up-to-date information that is designed to assist with all aspects of library work including management and administration, public services, reference, and technology. Includes a job board, directories of organizations and library and information specialists, reviews, recommendations, and links to some of the best subject-specific and "library" sites on the Web.

Minnesota E-Democracy (www.e-democracy.org/) is a nonpartisan citizen-based project whose mission is to improve participation in democracy in Minnesota through the use of information networks.

Morino Institute (www.morino.org/) is dedicated to opening the doors of opportunity—economic, civic, health, and education—and empowering people to improve their lives and communities in the communications age. The Institute helps individuals and institutions harness the power of information and the potential of interactive communications as tools for overcoming the challenges that face them. The Institute does not accept unsolicited proposals. Youth Advocacy and Services and Entrepreneurship are the Institute's two strategic areas of emphasis. The Social Networking area is more tactical in approach and the Institute will always have some degree of involvement in the Community Services area. Grants are normally made from the Morino Foundation, on behalf of the Institute, in support of initiatives or focus areas in which the Morino Institute is actively engaged. Grants are self-directed, done in partnership, and must be closely aligned to the Institute's mission. Its work is typically "program directed" and its funding is used to help evolve concepts or programs that it is incubating.

National Assembly of Local Arts Agencies (NALAA) (artsnet.heinz. cmu.edu/artsed/cs.nalaa.html) is a national organization specializing in up-to-date training, facts, peer networking, and maintaining a collective voice for local arts agencies and the arts at the community level. It is the professional organization for local arts agency administrators.

National Center for Nonprofit Boards (NCNB) (www.ncnb.org/) is a nonprofit organization dedicated to building stronger nonprofit boards and stronger nonprofit organizations. It exists to help nonprofit leaders—board members and paid executive staff—engineer healthy, powerful organizations. Its resources, leadership tools, and answers are designed to help you be a better nonprofit leader.

National Community Building Network (NCBN) (www.ncbn.org/) is an alliance of locally driven urban initiatives working to reduce poverty and create social and economic opportunity through comprehensive community-building strategies. Online resources include The Community Builder's Guide to Telecommunications Technology; a hyperlinked resource directory to lists and databases about individuals, organizations, and documents that can inform your community-building work; and an annotated bibliography on articles, papers, and books related to community building.

National Federation of Community Broadcasters (NFCB) (soundprint.org/~nfcb/) is a national membership organization of community-oriented noncommercial radio stations. Large and small, rural and urban, eclectic or targeted toward specific ethnic communities, the membership is distinguished by its localism and its community participation and support.

National Learning Object Standard Project (www.nlc-bnc.ca/ifla/II/metadata.htm) aims to standardize electronic information so that it can be retrieved from and combined with any other electronic information.

National Telephone Cooperative Association (www.ntca.org/), "The Voice of Rural Telecommunications" is a nonprofit association representing nearly five hundred small, rural telephone cooperatives and commercial companies. NTCA is a full-service association offering a wide array of member services.

The Nonprofit Center (www.fundsnetservices.com/nonproct.htm) provides information on resources for nonprofit organizations on the Internet. Includes a comprehensive directory of foundations, funding organizations, and corporate philanthropy programs.

Nonprofit Prophets (www.kn.pacbell.com/wired/prophets/) is an interactive project that challenges groups of students to investigate a problem that they see in the world and then create a Web resource page that teaches the world about the problem.

Nonprofit Technology Resources (www.libertynet.org/~ntr/) provides computer consulting, hands-on training, and telephone support to over two hundred nonprofit organizations annually in the Greater Philadelphia region.

Nonprofit.net (www.nonprofit.net/) brings together not-for-profit groups who are looking for a high-quality, low-cost solution to maintaining an online presence.

North Carolina Community Information Gateway (www.ncexchange.org/gateway/) links a variety of statewide programs from eight different viewpoints or "gateways." It is designed to support cross-issue collaboration and help North Carolina organizations and citizens use the Internet strategically to solve community problems.

North Carolina Community Resource Information System (CRIS) (www.cris.state.nc.us) is designed to be a customer-focused electronic resource on government programs and services. The North Carolina Office of State Planning, the Division of Community Assistance (N.C. Department of Commerce), the State Library of North Carolina, the Office of State Budget and Management, and other organizations have joined together to develop a system that will help local communities obtain information about state government technical and financial assistance programs and services.

OCLC Institute (www.oclc.org/institute/index.htm) is a nonprofit educational organization dedicated to promoting the evolution of libraries and information services by providing managers with opportunities for advanced education and knowledge exchange.

OCLC Online Computer Library Center (www.oclc.org) is a nonprofit, membership, library computer service and research organization dedicated to the public purposes of furthering access to the world's information and reducing information costs.

Old North End Community/Technology Center (homepages. together.net/~onectc5/) is a nonprofit, HUD-funded Enterprise Community program based in Burlington, Vermont. Its mission is to provide economic and cultural opportunities of the Information Age to neighborhood residents.

OMB Watch (ombwatch.org/ombwatch.html) is a nonprofit research, educational, and advocacy organization that focuses on budget, regulatory, nonprofit advocacy, and information policy. OMB Watch cochairs several coalitions in these issue areas and uses electronic communications technology to collect and disseminate policy information on such issues to community groups across the nation.

Plugged In (www.pluggedin.org/) was founded to bridge the technological gap between East Palo Alto and the Silicon Valley. Located just a few miles from the heart of Silicon Valley, East Palo Alto is an ethnically diverse low-income community of 25,000 that has been largely left behind in the economic boom that has transformed neighboring communities in the past decades. Plugged In offers a broad range of technology-related services that allows all people in this community to take advantage of the educational and economic opportunities created by information technologies.

Preparing Canada for a Digital World: Final Report of the Information Highway Advisory Council (strategis.ic.gc.ca/SSG/ih01650e. html) This detailed report provides background information on many information policies—applied to Canadian society. Chapters include Toward a Society Built on Knowledge; Access, Content, Jobs and Growth; Lifelong Learning and the Workplace; Government as a Model User; and the Road to the Future. This site also includes links to a variety of reports relative to the emerging use of the Internet in daily life.

RAMS-FIE (www.rams-fie.com) is a diversified information services company providing a full range of database services, software development, and technical support to the government, private sector, and academic communities. RAMS-FIE is the major link in the electronic transfer of information between research and educational organizations and the federal government.

The Right to Know Network (rtk.net) is a free, online network providing free access to numerous databases, text files, and conferences on the environment, housing, and sustainable development.

SeniorNet (www.seniornet.org/) is a national nonprofit organization whose mission is to build a community of computer-using seniors. SeniorNet provides adults age fifty-five and older with information and instruction about computer technologies so that they can use their new skills for their own benefit and to benefit society. SeniorNet has helped start over a hundred technology centers around the United States where computer classes specifically designed for older adults are offered. About half of SeniorNet's members are students or volunteers at the Learning Centers; the other half are independent members who participate through SeniorNet's electronic community, SeniorNet Online. SeniorNet also publishes computer-related materials for members, holds national conferences, and conducts research on the uses of technology by older adults. Of particular interest is *Older Adults and Computers: Report of a National Survey,* by Richard P. Adler (San Francisco: SeniorNet, 1996).

Technology Resource Consortium (TRC) (www.igc.apc.org/trc/) is a national organization of computer professionals dedicated to assisting nonprofits.

Telecom Information Resources on the Internet (www.spp.umich.edu/telecom/) contains references to information sources relating to the technical, economic, public policy, and social aspects of telecommunications. All forms of telecommunication, including voice, data, video, wired, wireless, cable TV, and satellite, are included. The intent is to provide pointers to other Web servers, with a brief description of the type of information. This list is maintained by Professor Jeff MacKie-Mason and Juan Riveros and is supported by the School of Public Policy and the School of Information at the University of Michigan.

Telecommunities Canada (www.tc.ca) is Canada's community networking association, which was formed to represent and promote the Canadian community networking movement at the national and international level and to ensure that all Canadians are able to participate in community-based communications and electronic information services by promoting and supporting local community network initiatives.

U.S. Department of Housing and Urban Development (HUD) (www.hud.gov/) supports computing learning centers in public and assisted housing through its Campuses of Learning, Neighborhood Networks, Safe Neighborhood Action Program (SNAP), and other initiatives.

Virtual University (www.vu.org) provides free online training classes about the Internet, technology, and other topics.

Volunteer Computer Corps (VCC) (www.engin.umich.edu/soc/vcc/) was started in 1993 and aims to fulfill the information services needed by nonprofit groups and schools. Since many charitable groups and schools lack the funds or the technical resources to support their computer related activities, VCC members volunteer to supplement their needs, free of charge.

Web Networks (www.Web.net) is a nonprofit organization dedicated to serving the electronic communications needs of the social change community in Canada.

Selected References

Beath, Cynthia M. "Supporting the Information Technology Champion." *MIS Quarterly* 15, no. 3 (September 1991): 355–72.

Beckley, Rika, Margaret A. Elliott, and Jeanine M. Prickett. "Closing the Gap: Information Technology and the Nonprofit Sector." *Nonprofit World* 14, no. 1 (January/February 1996): 36–42.

Bennis, Warren, and Patricia W. Biederman. *Organizing Genius: The Secrets of Creative Collaboration.* Reading, Mass.: Addison-Wesley, 1997.

Bobo, Kim, Jackie Kendall, and Steve Max. *Organizing for Social Change: A Manual for Activists in the 1990s.* Washington, D.C.: Seven Locks Press, 1991.

Carroll, John M., and Mary Beth Rosson. "Developing the Blacksburg Electronic Village." *Communications of the ACM* 39, no. 12 (December 1996): 69–75.

Chase, Timothy S. "Characterizations of Free-Nets in the United States and Canada: Facing History and Managing the Future." In *Connectedness: Information, Systems, People, Organizations; Proceedings of the 23rd Annual Conference, Canadian Association of Information Science.* Edmonton, Alberta, Canada: School of Library & Information Studies, University of Alberta, 1995.

Cisneros, Henry G. "The Public Interest, the Greater Good: How Government Should Work." *Journal of Housing and Community Development* 54, no. 2 (May/June 1997): 26–33.

Coleman, Pat. "Widening the Vision: Improving Access to Information, Part 2." *The Assistant Librarian* 89, no. 2 (February 1996): 20–21.

Connors, Tracy Daniel, ed. *The Nonprofit Organization Handbook,* 2nd ed. New York: McGraw-Hill, 1988.

Drucker, Peter F. *Managing the Non-Profit Organization.* New York: HarperCollins, 1990.

Dugan, Margret A. "Participatory and Empowerment Evaluation: Lessons Learned in Training and Technical Assistance. In David M. Fetterman, Shakeh J. Kaftarian, and Abraham Wandersman (eds.), *Empowerment Evaluation: Knowledge and Tools for Self-Assessment and Accountability.* Thousand Oaks, Calif.: Sage Publications, 1996.

Estabrook, Leigh. "Emerging Trends in Community Library Services." In Jane Robbins-Carter, ed., *Public Librarianship: A Reader,* 538–47. Littleton, Colo.: Libraries Unlimited, 1982.

Fetterman, David M., Shakeh J. Kaftarian, and Abraham Wandersman, eds. *Empowerment Evaluation: Knowledge and Tools for Self-Assessment and Accountability.* Thousand Oaks, Calif.: Sage Publications, 1996.

Fisher, Robert. *Let the People Decide: Neighborhood Organizing in America, Updated Edition.* New York: Twayne, 1994.

Glaser, Mark. "Grabbing for a Piece of Local Pie." *New Media* 7, no. 12 (September 22, 1997): 20+.

Greer, Roger C., and Martha L. Hale. "The Community Analysis Process." In Jane Robbins-Carter (ed.), *Public Librarianship: A Reader,* 358–66. Littleton, Colo.: Libraries Unlimited, 1982.

Grimley, Ben. "Service Without the Seams." In Service to the Citizen, *Government Technology* supplement, 10, no. 11 (October, 1997): 19+.

Gross, M. J., R. F. Larkin, R. S. Bruttomesso, and J. J. McNally. *Financial and Accounting Guide for Non-Profit Organizations.* New York: Wiley, 1995.

Guerena, Salvador. "Community Analysis and Needs Assessment." In Salvador Guerena (ed.), *Latino Librarianship: A Handbook for Professionals.* Jefferson, N.C.: McFarland, 1990.

Hammitt, Harry. "A Presumption of Openness." In Service to the Citizen, *Government Technology* supplement, 10, no. 11 (October 1997): 23+.

Harris, Blake. "The Quantum Mirror—Tomorrow's Paradigm." In Service to the Citizen, *Government Technology* supplement, 10, no. 11 (October 1997): 35–37.

Jones, Jennifer. "Tapping TIIAP." *Civic.com* (September 1997). (http://www.fcw-civic.com/pubs/sept/funding.htm)

Kahn, Si. *Organizing: A Guide for Grassroots Leaders.* New York: McGraw-Hill, 1982.

Kanter, Rosabeth Moss. *The Change Masters.* New York: Simon & Schuster, 1983.

Kelly, Maurie C. "Profiling a City: Information Resources on Chicago's 77 Community Areas." *Journal of Government Information* 23, no. 1 (January/February 1996): 1–11.

Kouzes, James M., and Barry Z. Posner. *The Leadership Challenge: How to Get Extraordinary Things Done in Organizations.* San Francisco: Jossey-Bass, 1987.

"Mark Merrifield's Entrepreneurial Approach to Public Librarianship." *InfoManage: The International Management Newsletter for the Information Professional* 2, no. 1 (December 1994): 1–3.

Mattessich, Paul W., and Barbara R. Monsey. *Collaboration: What Makes It Work.* Saint Paul, Minn.: Amherst H. Wilder Foundation, 1992.

Maxwell, Allison. "Service to the Citizen by the Citizen." In Service to the Citizen, *Government Technology* supplement, 10, no. 11 (October 1997): 6+.

Mayer, Steven E. "Building Community Capacity with Evaluation Activities That Empower." In David M. Fetterman, Shakeh J. Kaftarian, and Abraham Wandersman (eds.), *Empowerment Evaluation: Knowledge and Tools for Self-Assessment and Accountability.* Thousand Oaks, Calif.: Sage Publications, 1996.

McGarigle, Bill. "How to Finance 'Service to the Citizen' Projects." In Service to the Citizen, *Government Technology* supplement, 10, no. 11 (October 1997): 29–34.

Menzel, Donald C. "Governing the American County in the Twenty-First Century." *Spectrum* 69, no. 3 (summer 1996): 48–55.

Miller, Steven E. *Civilizing Cyberspace: Policy, Power, and the Information Superhighway.* Reading, Mass.: Addison-Wesley, 1996.

Mitchell, Mark A., and Donald Yates. "How to Attract and Retain the Best Volunteers." *Nonprofit World* 14, no. 4 (July/August 1996): 47–48.

Morino, Mario. *Impact of Technology on Youth in the Twenty-First Century.* Reston, Va.: Morino Institute, 1997. (http://www.morino.org/about.impactoftech.html)

———. *Assessment and Evolution of Community Networking.* Reston, Va.: Morino Institute, 1994. (www.morino.org/publications/assessment.html)

Murray, Michael. "Evaluating Web Impact—the Death of the Highway Metaphor." *Direct Marketing* 59, no. 9 (January 1997): 36–39.

Newcombe, Tod. "If You Build It, Will They Come?" In Service to the Citizen, *Government Technology* supplement, 10, no. 11 (October 1997): 18–23.

———. "Tackling Mistrust with Technology." *Government Technology* supplement, 10, no. 11 (October 1997): 1+.

O'Connell, Brian. "A Major Transfer of Government Responsibility to Voluntary Organizations? Proceed with Caution." *Public Administration Review* 56, no. 3 (May/June 1996): 222–25.

Pearson, Glenice B. "Is It Time for a Paradigm Shift on Volunteers?" *Fund Raising Management* 27, no. 6 (August 1996): 12–13.

Pettigrew, Karen E., and Margaret A. Wilkinson. "Controlling the Quality of Community Information: An Analysis of the Effects on Dissemination of the Differences Between I&R Agencies and Community Networks." *Information and Referral* 16 (1994): 185–94.

Pungitore, Verna L. *Innovation and the Public Library: The Adoption of New Ideas in Public Libraries.* Westport, Conn.: Greenwood Press, 1995.

Rapp, Melissa A., and Rona Wotschak. "Partnerships: the Prescription for Healthier Communities." *Journal of Health Care Marketing* 16, no. 4 (winter 1996): 43–44.

Robbins, Harvey. *Turf Wars: Moving from Competition to Collaboration.* Glenview, Ill.: Scott, Foresman, 1990.

South Carolina State Development Board. *A Guide to Community Analysis.* Columbia, S.C.: Community Analysis and Development Division, South Carolina State Development Board, 1990.

Stern, Gary J. *Marketing Workbook for Nonprofit Organizations.* Saint Paul, Minn.: Amherst H. Wilder Foundation, 1990.

Trinidad, Jeremy S. "Information and Referral in the One-Stop Paradigm." *Information and Referral* 18 (1996): 41–66.

Tucker, Lorene, and James Nelson. "Information and Referral in Dallas County." *Show-Me Libraries* 44, no. 1 (fall 1992): 43–44.

Wedgeworth, Robert. "Prospects for and Effecting Change in the Public Library." In Jane Robbins-Carter (ed.), *Public Librarianship: A Reader.* Littleton, Colo.: Libraries Unlimited, 1982.

Whitehead, Derek. "Government Policy: Leading or Following?" *Australian Library Review* 13, no. 3 (August 1996): 257–68.

Winer, Michael, and Karen Ray. *Collaboration Handbook: Creating, Sustaining, and Enjoying the Journey.* Saint Paul, Minn.: Amherst H. Wilder Foundation, 1994.

Woods, Deb. "The I&R Heart of Community-wide Networks: HelpNet, a Model under Construction." *Information and Referral* 18 (1996): 7–19.

Zander, Alvin. *Making Groups Effective,* 2nd ed. San Francisco: Jossey-Bass, 1994.

Index

Porter, Jeanne, 84–85
press releases, 123
price in marketing, 121
primary public in marketing, 121
process evaluation, 170
process factor in partnerships, 67–68
products in marketing, 120
Promoting Community Change
(Homan), 29
promotional campaigns in marketing,
121–25
proposals. *See* grant writing
PSAs (public service announcements),
123
public access workstations, 147–65. *See
also* access
examples of, 149–59
funding, 147–48
ideas on, 161–62
information resources on, 147–49,
163–65
overview of, 19, 147
training and technical help for,
159–60
public relations. *See* marketing
Public Sector Continuous
Improvement Site, 87
public service announcements (PSAs),
123
publics in marketing, 121
purpose factors in partnerships, 68

R
Rankin Inlet, Northwest Territories,
example, 156–57
Ray, Karen, 69, 169
"Reinventing Citizenship: The Practice
of Public Work" report, 59–60
resources factors in partnerships, 68
resources, financial. *See* funding
resources, information. *See* information resources; Web sites
results evaluation, 168, 170
River Systems Web site, 90
Rouyn-Noranda, Quebec, example,
157–58

S
Sakku Arctic Technologies, 157
Schuler, Douglas, 31, 32–33, 70
Seattle Community Network mission
statement, 38
secondary public in marketing, 121
SEFLIN (Southeast Florida Library
Information Network) Free-Net,
37–38, 50
services. *See also* community network-
ing services
Information and Referral services,
28, 138–40
of United Ways, 137–38
Smart Communities, 33, 87
Snowe-Rockefeller Amendment, 4–5
SOLINET (Southeast Library
Network) example, 140–43
Southeastern Alberta example, 158–59
standardizing local online information, 141–43
startup costs, 99–101
State and Local Government on the
Net, 87
States Inventory Project, 87
steering committees, 39–41
Stern, Gary J., 118, 120, 122, 123, 124
strategic information systems, 23–24
structure factor in partnerships,
67–68

T
Tallahassee Free-Net example, 50, 114,
132–33
TCFN (Columbia Free-Net), 71
technical help services, 19–20, 159–60
Technology Resource Institute (TRI),
165
telecommunications policy, 3–5
Telecommunications Reform Act of
1996, 4
text-based information formats, 42–44
TGCI (Grantsmanship Center),
111–12
Thompson, Jennifer, 75
Three Rivers Free-Net (TRFN) example, 15, 50, 72, 94, 131–32

Stephen T. Bajjaly is an assistant professor in the College of Library and Information Science at the University of South Carolina where he teaches information technology and management courses. He is also a founder and the project director of MidNet, the local community network that is sponsored by the College. Bajjaly received his Ph.D. in information science from the State University of New York at Albany, an M.B.A. in information systems from San Diego State University, and a B.S. in psychology from St. Lawrence University.